SOCIAL WORK AT GRADY HOSPITAL:

CHALLENGES AND REWARDS

SOCIAL WORK AT GRADY HOSPITAL: CHALLENGES AND REWARDS

CHARLENE TURNER, editor

ISBN: 9798589510560
©2020 Charlene Turner
All Rights Reserved

Printed in the United States of America

FOREWORD

"THE GRADYS" was an Atlanta institution founded in 1892. It was the "charity" hospital for the two counties that then made up Atlanta: Fulton and Dekalb County. The official name was Henry W. Grady Memorial Hospital, named for a Southern progressive journalist, who championed the building of a medical facility for the poor. Henry Grady would also have a high school and a university school of journalism named in his honor. Despite its proper name, the hospital was called "the Gradys" because it was segregated and was in effect, one hospital for Whites and one for African-Americans. Even when they built the new hospital in the 1940's, it was in the shape of a giant H with Blacks on one side and Whites on the other. The hospital was integrated in 1959, but the name stuck.

Emma Thomas, MSW, was born and raised in Monroe, Georgia about one-hour east of Atlanta. In the late 1940's and early 1950's she earned a bachelor's degree from Spellman College and a master's degree from the Atlanta University School of Social Work. As if this wasn't quite an achievement for a Black woman at that time, she was also hired as the first Black social worker at the Grady's.

In the mid 1960's Miss Thomas was asked to become the Director of the Social Service Department but declined because she felt she would not be taken seriously. Miss Thomas had a very realistic view of life and was no nonsense about the effects of racial prejudice in and out of the workplace. Instead, she took the position of assistant director and this was her role when I was hired as a medical social worker in 1969.

Miss Thomas was the epitome of dignity and deportment. She was probably about 5' 3' but she carried herself so regally she appeared much taller. She weighed about 130 lbs., had neck-length jet-black hair with a touch of gray, and always dressed in well-made professional dresses and suits. Over her clothes she wore a white lab coat whether meeting patients in her office, the clinics, or on the inpatient areas. Since, at that time, there were very few Black employees; Miss Thomas told us that without the lab coat she was often mistaken for a member of the maintenance department.

Miss Thomas was a consummate professional. She would get straight to the heart of an issue. She was a no-nonsense person who told you what she thought without qualification. She became the role model for the evolving professional self of so many young social workers.

As a supervisor, Miss Thomas was incredible. Two of her former supervisees attest to her ability:

Dorothy F. Carrillo

I

Nothing could have prepared this Midwest Omaha girl for the Grady experience. Miss Thomas was my mentor for sure. At my first introduction, she told me I could ask her any question ... once. So, when I went to her with the same question several months later she reminded me that I had already asked that one. She was wise, educated, and most importantly embedded in the community. The patients respected her and she respected them. That attribute was essential and she passed it on to me.

The doctors pushed us to get patients out. I remember one particularly difficult gentleman with nowhere to go. Miss Thomas helped me by calling the owner of the grocery store on his street corner (she knew him). He took the man home with him. I was assigned to orthopedics. If my patients didn't have shoes, she found me a way to get some for them (without paper work).

Long before the Coronavirus, she kept her office immaculately clean and wiped her phone down on a regular basis. She made me laugh by telling me that I should not eat any food that was given to me as a gift (she absolutely would not) saying, "You never know Mrs. H."

Diana H

II

I guess my lasting memory of Miss Thomas was her professionalism and her lesson that I call SW101 ..."starting where the client is." I was a very green social worker right out of graduate school when I went to work at Grady in March of 1970. I would go up to the floors that were assigned to me and come back and report to Miss Thomas. I would say, "The head nurse wants me to do this or the doctor wants me to do that" and Miss Thomas would say, "What does the patient want?"

On behalf of the many social workers whose lives she touched and taught what it means to be a professional, we thank you, Emma Thomas, and dedicate this book to you.

Olivia H.

TABLE OF CONTENTS

Acknowledgements i
Introduction ii

SOCIAL WORK INTERVENTION: GRADY STYLE

Hurricane Katrina 1
My "Special Patients" 4
Special Moments In Memorable Cases 10
Lost and Found 13
Ambulatory Clinic 16
Patients Taught Me 18

IT ALL HAPPENS IN THE ER

Grady Memories, The ER, and the Olympics 25
Knowing The Death Script All too Well 34
The Right of Choice 37
Code Triage 40
Meet The Disaster Junkies 44
Emergency Room Memories 48

EVERYTHING I NEEDED TO KNOW: BUT DID NOT LEARN IN SOCIAL WORK SCHOOL

Closing Grady's Dialysis Clinic 56
My Life As A Social Work Administrator 61
Game Changer Moments and Events 67
Gentrification Atlanta Style 75
Reflections: The Metamorphosis of a Neophyte 77
I Am Only Staying Six Years ... And Eighteen Years Later 88
Social Work Is My Second Career 91
Hajib Episode 93

CONTENTS

UNSUNG HEROES IN SPECIALTY AREAS

Social Work DNA	96
Resilience	100
Tales From The Grady Surgical Intensive Care	104
HIV/Aids Social Work at Grady	107
Making A Case For Advocacy	115
Life in the Day of a Grady Social Worker	119
Geriatric Clinic	122
Experiences with Pediatric Services	124
A Unique Group Experience	127
The Need For A Social Admit	136
Mental Illness or Just Human?	139

POSTSCRIPT

The Miracle Workers	141
Heaven's Angels	145

CONTRIBUTORS   150

ACKNOWLEDGEMENTS

If I haven't done so before, I would be remiss to pass on this opportunity to acknowledge my family. I truly thank my two daughters because there was sacrifice on their part as their mom was almost always "on-call" to Grady. Thank you Johnetta. Thank you Angela. And, thanks to my two grandchildren, Angel and Anderson, who likewise, learned to share "granny".

Special thanks to Ed Renford, former CEO, Curtis Lewis, MD. former Medical Director, Howard Mosby, Vice President, and Tim Jefferson, SVP, Legal Affairs- along with the many others who supported us over the years. I worked closely with many of my supervisors for decades and developed lifelong friends—and of course you know who you are. Doll Adams, James Reed, Jim Hammons and Maranda Randolph deserve a special shoutout! I am also grateful for the enduring support from the medical staff; several of them deserve special mention, Dr. James McCoy, Dr. Bill Sexson, Dr. Maura George, Dr. Charles Moore, Dr. Micheal Lubin —and most notably, the late Dr. Ken Walker who was our loudest champion.

Lastly, but not last at all, I want to thank all of the Grady social workers, my entire staff over the years. I couldn't reach out to all. Thank you to my contributors who wrote articles in this book. Thank you for sharing a few of your memories and giving a glimpse, a tidbit of our many efforts to help make this world a better place. There is no way I could have singly provided the depth and richness of these collective memories of our time at Grady.

My gratitude to Estella Moore, a dear friend and colleague, who patiently worked with me through the editing and publishing process. And, thanks to all who have offered words of encouragement along the way.

INTRODUCTION

Grady Hospital, (now known as the Grady Health System) is one of the largest public hospitals in the Southeast and is well known for its trauma care. A common refrain throughout the Atlanta community is: "If I am hurt in a bad accident or in a critical condition – take me to Grady." However, in more recent years, the topnotch care provided in some other programs has also gained recognition: the Burn Center, the Stroke Center, the Cancer Center, the Infectious Disease Program, the Primary Care Center –to name just a few. The medical staff comes from Emory University and the Morehouse School of Medicine which features some of the country's leading physicians.

During most of my tenure, the hospital operated under major financial strain. However, I am told that in recent years the hospital has made a resounding rebound in its financial situation under the leadership of the current CEO, John Haupert, and its present corporate board.

The idea of writing this book started with my retirement after 40 years at Grady Hospital, when I announced at one of my retirement parties that I was going to write a book. I made that statement in 2013 and now during this time of the Coronavirus Pandemic and sheltering in place in 2020, I decided to start a book-writing project. In thinking about how to get started, I contacted the workers I could easily reach – and many eagerly took on the task of writing their chapters.

Social work at Grady is unique in the challenges it presents, but rewarding in the sense that so much can be accomplished in offering a helping hand to patients who are hurting in so many ways. We want the readers to visualize our stories and gain a glimpse of what we faced on a daily basis. The stories that follow will provide snapshots of what each worker carries in their memory bank about their "Grady Days." The editing is minimal, so you can sample the many flavors of this pallet of diverse races, ethnicities, cultures, and genders that made up the Grady Social Service Department under my tenure.

It has been said—if you can work at Grady, you can work successfully anywhere. It is true that social work at Grady provided daily challenges that refined and defined one's skills as a social work practitioner. To work in this setting was a constant test of one's social work values and ethics as we strived to provide the best possible service to an underserved patient population. We often had to create or manufacture our own resources in our world of limited resources. Luckily, the department had access to an "emergency fund" which could be utilized to meet the needs of patients when community resources were not readily available. It should be noted that there was never a dull moment in this environment as we wore many "hats" – one minute we might be counseling a dying patient and in the next minute dealing with an abandoned elderly person or a simple transportation problem. It was all in a day's work of fulfilling our mission as social workers: To meet the needs of our patients to the best of our ability.

We are pleased to provide a picture of social work from this perspective. Some of the articles included in this book will be didactic in nature; others may be somewhat amusing—but they will all touch your heart as you will experience what it means to minister to those in need. Each writer was asked to present what he or she held in their memory bank from their days at the hospital; some wrote about patients they will never forget and others wrote about events that have stayed with them.

Finally, as you read this book, I hope you get a sense of the dedication and commitment of these workers. I owe all of them a debt of gratitude for helping me build a department known for its advocacy and quality service to patients. I also want to thank the larger hospital community for believing in social work and validating our contribution to the hospital.

Charlene Turner

SOCIAL WORK INTERVENTION:

GRADY STYLE

HURRICANE KATRINA

Louise Spiro

In 2005, Hurricane Katrina hit the Gulf Shore destroying the city of New Orleans. Thousands of people lost everything and many lost their lives. As people started fleeing the destroyed city, many found their way to Atlanta. Those seeking medical care found their way to Grady Hospital. With them came incredible stories of survival. People talked about harrowing stories of destruction. People losing everything they had. Others talked about the loss of life. One man told me about how he was on the roof of his home for two days before he was rescued. One lady I worked with had a story that has stayed with me until this day.

Anne was an 82-year-old widow who suffered from diabetes and was bought to Grady hospital by her son. He was worried about his mother, as she had not had her insulin for almost a week. She was a refugee from this hurricane which destroyed her home as well as her city of New Orleans. This short somewhat plump woman said little but her eyes told her story. You could see the fear and sadness in them. As the doctor began examining her and ordering proper medications, I checked the clothes closet for clothes for her and the toiletries she needed.

The time came when I was able to talk to Anne alone. At first, she did not want to talk about her experience but I encouraged her to tell her story. She said she and her 80-year-old sister lived in senior housing and when it was announced that the storm was coming and everyone had to evacuate, she didn't know what to do. She did not have a car and had relied on public transportation for her needs. She had no way to leave the city. When the mayor told her that there would be shelter in the Superdome, she and her sister followed the directions given to them and went to the Superdome. They felt they would be safe there as the building was large and the mayor said they would be safe. Throughout her narrative, she continues to repeat that they followed the directions of the mayor.

The first day wasn't bad but as the building started to fill up, it became apparent that they were not really prepared for the number of people entering the building. Each day that went by, the conditions became worst as the area became more and more crowded. Anne talked about being hungry and thirsty as there wasn't enough food nor water. She for sure was not able to maintain her diabetic diet. There weren't enough toilets and after a few days all the toilets became backed up and the smell in the building was unbearable coupled with the heat, as there was no air-conditioning.

Then the building began flooding from the rain outside. She then talked about how scared she and her sister became as people began getting raped and robbed of the few possessions that people had brought with them. She then looked as if she would cry but didn't as she told me what happened. She was sitting next to a young mother with two little babies who were crying, as they were hungry. Anne took the 2-year-old into her arms to help this mother. As she rocked her in her arms, the baby stopped crying and she continued to rock the toddler. At one point, she noticed the baby went limp and she thought the girl had finally fallen asleep. The child had died in her arms.

Still tears did not come, rather a faraway look came to her face. Anne continued. After five days of "hell" she said that she and her sister were put on a bus and taken to Houston, Texas where they were hurdled into the Astrodome. They were hungry and thirsty, for all they were given on the bus ride was peanut butter crackers. Also, it had been five days without her insulin.

Finally, the two women were able to contact Anne's son who lived in Atlanta. He came and drove them to Atlanta where he took her to Grady. After she finally told her story, she sat quietly for a while and then the tears began slowly at first. Then her tears and sobs became louder. I held her and she began to wail for what appeared to be an infinite amount of time. When she finally stopped, she admitted that this was the first time she had cried since the whole nightmare began. This was the first time she had felt safe enough to cry.

These were the tears that Anne needed to start healing after the terrible trauma that she had just experienced. The doctor had treated her medically to stabilize her diabetes. Grady was able to provide her with the medications she needed, as well as some of the concrete personal needs. Most of all, she received the emotional "first aid" to start over.

MY "SPECIAL" PATIENTS

Charlene Turner

Mr. C was a self-referred patient who came to Social Service to get a shelter referral. He wanted a referral to a particular shelter and even proceeded to tell me what I should write in the referral. I decided to make him "earn" this referral since he was so "smart." I wanted his history and some idea of how he ended up homeless. He had worked the "docks" in Alabama for many years, but the dock was closed and he came to Atlanta in the hope of finding work. (I later learned that substance abuse was a factor in his unemployment). He was feeling defeated at this point—but I was able to determine that he did not want to continue living in a shelter. He wanted to work - so he was immediately referred to Personnel (and I called ahead of time to prepare the way for him). I completed an application for him and within a week, he was a Grady employee in the Housekeeping Department (again, I called in a favor).

He had worked in Housekeeping for many years when he proudly came in the office one day to tell me he was "moving up" to become an OR tech. He got married and began a whole new chapter in his life. Were there bumps in the road over the years-absolutely! His wife even called me at one point and requested that I "talk" to him as he was drinking again. Of course, his job performance was affected and he would have lost his job without the support he received from the Employee Advocate, Pauline Farris, and myself. He finally agreed to go to an inpatient program at the Salvation Army and I attended his graduation months later. I might mention that he began to refer a number of his "street buddies" to me with the promise that I could get them jobs at Grady —so I had to stop those referrals. To my knowledge, he is still employed at the hospital.

Ms. B was a thirty-year-old patient who was admitted to the hospital due to ingestion of lye. She was one of my first patients. She expressed much anger towards the medical staff for having saved her life. She would even throw things at them and greet them with some pretty profane words. She never threw things at me—but was most difficult and would barely talk to me or even look at me. She was despondent over a bad breakup with her boyfriend and despite my best efforts, I seemingly could not get her to be more hopeful.

Approximately ten years or so later as I walked down Butler Street (now called Jesse Hill), a lady approached me and asked if I remembered her. She looked vaguely familiar, but I was not sure who she was. The lady was Ms. B who told me she knew she was "pretty mean" when she was in the hospital. She expressed gratitude for Grady having saved her life and said she was glad we never gave up on her. Of course, this encounter made my day and reminded me that sometimes we don't immediately see the results of our work—but we still have to give our best effort.

Mr. R was referred because he needed help in getting his disability application approved. He was in his late 50s' and had a severe case of gout along with some other medical problems. He was a meek, rather shy gentleman who initially revealed little about himself. I learned that he had a 20+ year work history at a local hotel but was now physically limited and unable to do the work. He needed a desk job, but that was not possible because he was illiterate. Given his work history, it was apparent that he did not wake up one morning and decide to be lazy. His physician was also convinced that Mr. R was unable to work-so he gave me a complete education of Mr. R's medical condition. Mr. R's case was already at the level of an administrative law judge-so we went to court with his medical records in hand and my newfound medical knowledge. Mr. R was so nervous he could hardly speak—so I spoke for him and his physician as well. Even though I provided my credentials when we arrived, I am convinced the judge thought I was a doctor. His disability application was approved and he continued to visit me over the years whenever he had important papers to be read.

My work with Mr. P led to the Secret Service calling me one afternoon. I was unnerved by this call-and after I gathered my wits I was able to convince the agent that my patient was incapable of harming the President who was about to visit Atlanta. Mr. P is the only patient I have ever encountered who preferred to live in the woods (in the wild from his definition). He had grown up in a facility in South Georgia that housed residents who were referred to as "retarded" at that time. He was naïve and childlike and not comfortable around a lot of people - but he had considerable knowledge about plants and trees. Periodically, he came to the hospital due to severe swelling and pain in his leg, the result of a bite by a rare spider. The doctors recommended amputation-but he adamantly refused. He traveled extensively from time to time, hitchhiking to odd places and on more than one occasion needed funds to get back to Georgia (remember we had an emergency fund). He did receive a Social Security check and on two occasions, he decided to return the funds stating that he did not need the money. I helped him get reinstated with Social Security each time-and finally helped him to understand that he should come to see me before he went to return his check again.

Mr. P was a veteran referred to me because he was homeless (seeing a homeless patient in the early 70s was a rarity). He was a native Georgian whose family had disowned him due to his alcoholism. Having worked in an alcohol treatment program in Chicago, I felt very capable of working with this patient. On my second visit to see the patent—the doctor had written in bold letters— "the patient does not want to see the social worker again." This was my assigned area and with my damaged ego, I proceeded to see the patient again—but with a very different approach. I took the time to get to know him and was amazed to learn that he spoke several languages, was very proud of his military record and he had always wanted to be a nurse. When he left the hospital, he was ready to go to the Salvation Army for rehab. He stayed for one year and I followed his progress. He proceeded to get training as a nurse's aide and began work at the hospital. He was such a success story that he was profiled in the Grady News at that time. Mr. P was one of only a few white patients I had at that time. We quickly got past our early hiccup and bonded around my expressed belief in his potential.

My history with Mr. W spans over twenty years —in fact, he used to call me "Ma." He had a difficult childhood-in and out of foster homes-much of which carried over into his adult life. In his early twenties, he suffered a gunshot to the head and suffered from seizures. Let me try to summarize this twenty-year history:

a. Homeless most of the time —when he needed shelter for a while, he readily acknowledged that he would "talk suicidal" and get himself admitted to Psychiatry.
b. On one of his many visits to the hospital, he encountered one of our hospital attorneys and told her he was my son. She was surprised to learn I had a son. I informed her that I had no son and that I certainly would not have had one that age.
c. Mr. W got married and Doll Adams and I attended his wedding and were introduced as his family. He was dressed in a tuxedo and acted like a perfect gentleman. The marriage lasted less than a year due to his drug use (as reported to me by his wife).
d. Mr. W decided to burglarize a house —he mistakenly picked the home of a police officer and ended up in prison for a few years. When the Christmas Holiday arrived, his social worker decided to send him a few dollars in a money order. I received a note back advising me not to send any more money as I was not authorized to do so. The money order was not returned.
e. Mr. W was referred to a supportive housing program. The Emergency Fund covered his initial payment and I actually went there on the day of his admission. Since he was known to everyone in the department —many of us had contributed many household items —we even found a microwave and a color TV. At this point, he is receiving a disability check and his rent was

in accordance with his income. He acted like he was moving into the White House and I fully expected him to be settled for some time. Within three months, he left the housing program, stating that they were taking too much of his money.

    f.   At one point, he became a Grady employee (helped by one of my allies) and he seemed to be doing well in his job in Housekeeping. Grady had a three-month probationary period at that time – and one or two days before his probation was over-he brought a gun to work and waved it at someone on an elevator. Immediate termination was in order- he pleaded and pleaded for another chance, to no avail.

He has been lost to follow up and I am told he no longer goes to Grady. Once before when he disappeared for a span of time —we found him by calling all the local jails. I have some suspicion that he is probably incarcerated again. His lifestyle was such that I made sure that I documented his next of kin in the record and explained to him why I felt the need to do so.

Many of you reading this book may wonder how and/or why I saw so many patients as an administrator. Well, there are two primary reasons. First of all, I was a social worker first and an administrator second. Secondly, I loved the patient contact and wanted to model for staff how to deal with patients and to also experience firsthand the challenges they had in meeting the needs of our patients.

The final chapter of this book is being done in the midst of the holiday season in 2020. So, I would be remiss if I did not mention another special patient. Mr. JW was a veteran who chose to get his medical care at Grady instead of the VA Hospital and he was having difficulty getting his disability approved after having being exposed to Agent Orange in Vietnam. His doctors gave him a grim prognosis and we were determined to help him get his disability approved. The necessary papers were completed and his disability was approved. This seemed to be a simple task-but it must have been a big deal for Mr. JW as he started sending a Xmas Card to the department with words of appreciation every year —approximately twenty years ago. He has continued to send me a card every year, even after my retirement and I have no idea how he obtained my home address. Needless to say, I now look forward to that Xmas card every year. Thank you, Mr. JW.

SPECIAL MOMENTS IN MEMORABLE CASES

Dollmeisha Adams

As I reflect on memorable cases, the most prominent is that of "Mr. W". Despite being wheelchair-bound, his large body stature was prominent. On more than one occasion, I witnessed him get out of his wheelchair supporting himself on bilateral stumps-and lift it onto the city transit bus. He was not at all shy of facing down someone with whom he disagreed. He was very capable of getting out of his wheelchair and engaging in a confrontational standoff with others.

He would sip the bottle on occasion and present with this sheepish grin when he knew that I knew he was a bit tipsy. We had a very positive relationship and he would make requests without reservation if he needed assistance. Those who did not know him very well would have likely described him as difficult or threatening. He never presented that side in our exchanges. Truth be told, I think that he viewed me as excessively respectable and rarely, if ever, presented what young folk would describe as "hood behavior." He knew that I would pursue services on his behalf.

On one occasion he had concerns relating to his "maleness" and lo and behold if he didn't roll into Ms. Charlene Turner's office, Director of Social Services, and present the concern to her instead of me.

II

Identifying next-of-kin for deceased patients was routine in earlier times and the task fell to the social worker for the assigned clinic or inpatient area. There were many cases of this kind. However, one stands out. During the period when common-law relationships gained some legal standing, a patient died who was in a common-law relationship.

However, his common-law wife had taken ill and had gone to live with her daughter. The patient was admitted rather suddenly and died, leaving the hospital with no information. Thankfully, the ambulance trip sheet did note the patient's address. Also, the common-law wife remained in touch and she and her daughter consented to meet me at the patient's home. I requested police presence and they accompanied me to the patient's home.

To put this in a broader perspective, the patient's home was filled with merchandise from the store he once owned, i.e., new stoves, refrigerators, typewriters and more. During our visit, a gentleman stopped by who had initiated a business proposition with the patient prior to his death. He mentioned that he would be following through via the court. The common-law wife and her daughter took note and followed through with the court system as well, with a positive outcome-if memory serves me correctly.

Sometime later there was a newspaper article, depicting a policeman kneeling with a GREAT deal of cash that was retrieved from this same patient's home as a result of a homeless person illegally entering the residence. The patient had a huge amount of cash at the residence, i.e., into the thousands of dollars. Legally, the common-law wife would be first-line recipient of the cash.

III

Current day race relations—with its many and varied reflections of our society—brings to mind a case dating back some 25 to 30 years ago. An elderly Black woman with identified family chose to name her white employer as her medical decision-maker. Her family was not pleased and I listened patiently to the family's displeasure with the decision. I don't recall any specific undesirable act on the family's part as an explanation for the patient's choice. A longstanding, trusting relationship with the employer appeared to be the basis for her decision.

At the family's request, I broached the discussion with the patient. She was oriented and remained steadfast. There was obviously a greater degree of trust in her employer than her family members.

I share this in light of today's complicated race issues and unrest. It reveals the simultaneous connectedness and unshakable trust between this patient and her white employer and her disconnection with her family.

LOST AND FOUND

Darcell Colbert

Mr. H was admitted to Grady Hospital in the summer of 2005, after the police found him wandering around the Greyhound Bus Station. He was admitted to 12A, the Morehouse Medicine Floor. According to the ER notes in the chart, Mr. H was found wandering, confused and his clothes smelled of urine. He had a wallet in his trouser pocket, which was entered into Security-Patient Valuables. He was diagnosed with dementia.

His physician asked me to see him for discharge planning. I interviewed him, and found him pleasantly confused, alert, and oriented to person only, speech slightly slurred and a poor historian. I had some difficulty understanding what he was trying to communicate because of his confusion. He was in two point restraints* for his own safety to prevent him from wandering. According to his nurse, he was independent with activities of daily living: bathing, dressing, and ambulation. He was also incontinent of bladder and bowel.

On his behalf, I began an investigation of Mr. H. I went to Security, specifically, Patient Valuables and requested his wallet to look through, in hopes of finding information such as his address and some leads to his family. Mr. H's identification card gave me his date of birth, showed him with a Fort Lauderdale, Florida address, and no telephone number. There was also a Medicare card in his wallet.

I contacted the Broward County Police Department, explained the situation, and requested a welfare check in hopes of finding his family. While awaiting the Broward County Police Department's response, I continued to see Mr. H

Usually a cloth device which is used to wrap around the waist and around the wrists to immobilize the arms.

daily, in hopes of obtaining any pertinent information. After two days passed, I heard back from the Broward County Police Department. The officer told me that no one answered the door, the grass was tall and the outside of the house needed repairs. The officer spoke with a few neighbors and learned Mr. H lived alone. According to them, someone picked him up on Sunday mornings and dropped him back home in the afternoon. The neighbors said on Sundays, he was dressed as if he was going to church, but they didn't know where.

I continued to see Mr. H daily and talk with him in hopes of obtaining pertinent information about him and where he attended church. After two weeks passed, the physician discontinued his restraints; however, he was placed on a one to one sitter. Over time, his cognitive status improved slightly and he mentioned the deacons in the church. I asked if he was a deacon in his church and the name of his church. There was no response from him to that. Another week passed, while I continued to see him every day and to ask him questions about his church. Finally, Mr. H mentioned Calvary Baptist Church. I looked up the name of Calvary Baptist Church in Fort Lauderdale, Florida on the internet in his zip code. I contacted Calvary Baptist Church in Fort Lauderdale, Florida, Broward County, and the pastor answered the telephone. I explained the situation and asked if he had a member by the name S. H. The pastor responded yes and told me he was one of their deacons at the church.

The pastor informed me that the other deacons had been looking for him for three weeks now. He told me that he would send four deacons to Atlanta, Georgia to pick up Mr. H and transport him back to Fort Lauderdale. The pastor told me Mr. H had no family; his wife died two years ago. I asked the Pastor to have the deacons bring Mr. H some clothes and shoes to wear.

On the day the deacons arrived, his physician, charge nurse, and I met with the deacons and informed them of Mr. H's cognitive status and that he is a wanderer. The deacons were aware of his dementia diagnosis; however, they were not aware that Mr. H had begun to wander. The physician explained to the deacons that Mr. H could not continue to live alone anymore. The deacons informed us that they have a church member who owns a group home and they could place Mr. H. there. Mr. H was discharged in the care of the deacons of Calvary Baptist Church with discharge paperwork, prescriptions, and his belongings.

AMBULATORY CLINIC

Valeria Beasley

I first met Ms. B in the Main Social Service Office at Grady Hospital. She presented to the office requesting to see the social worker for the Eye Clinic. The Eye Clinic is one of the many clinics that I covered during my tenure at Grady. Ms. B was seen in the Eye Clinic and given a prescription for eyeglasses. During this time, Social Service worked with the Georgia Lighthouse for the Blind providing vouchers to assist patients with purchasing eyeglasses. I met with Ms. B who was accompanied by her mother. To give a little background information on Ms. B, she was an African American female in her early twenties. She requested assistance with purchasing her eyeglasses, I tried to explain to her that we did not have any vouchers at that time to assist her with obtaining her eyeglasses. Ms. B got upset after I informed her that I did not know when we would get new vouchers. She abruptly stood up and left the office yelling, "I bet if I had blonde hair and blue eyes, you would help me." Her mother stated, "That's right, you are not going to deny my daughter what's rightfully hers." Ms. B's mother left the office.

Approximately 10 minutes later I received a phone call from the hospital administrator's office stating that Ms. B and her mother were in their office complaining that I refused to help her. I had to explain to administration what I said. This was one of many encounters that I had with Ms. B throughout the years. At different times she would open up and go into details about herself.

On different occasions, Ms. B would come to see me requesting something to eat or assistance with transportation to get home. At this time, we would provide patients with a bag lunch if they had been to the hospital for an extended period of time. Ms. B would get off the Marta bus asking for something to eat and a bus token (Marta used bus tokens, this was before Breeze Cards). Ms. B felt entitled, she often stated that her father was a construction worker and, "He helped renovate this hospital." When I refused to give her a bag lunch or a bus token, she often ended up complaining to administration and she and I would go backward and forward daily. She would often request a referral to go to a local church to get clothes. Once I brought her some clothes that I bought and never wore. She left the clothes in the Social Service office, stating that she didn't want them, "because they was cheap and old." She would come to the hospital every other day for no reason.

I eventually developed a short-term relationship with Ms. B and her mother. Ms. B's mother confided in me that she used to work with young children until she started having medical issues. Her mother was hoping that she would one day be able to go back to work. Ms. B has never been married and has no children. She lives with her mother in a 2-bedroom apartment in the projects (public housing apartments). Ms. B has an older brother and younger sister. She graduated from high school and went to job corps, she never answered whether she graduated from the program. She has worked as a teacher's assistant for Head Start.

I later encountered Ms. B as the social worker in the Asthma Clinic and Medical Clinic. She had been discharged from both clinics due to making false accusations against both physicians. One physician was accused of tearing her clothes. However, her mother was present the entire visit. She would contact me to convince the physician to allow her to continue receiving treatment from both physicians. Later, her mother informed me that before coming to Grady, she had been discharged from a previous clinic facility for the same behavior.

Ms. B refused referrals to be evaluated by Psychiatry, even though she had a family history of depression and schizophrenia. Eventually, she became abusive and violent with her mother. She has been incarcerated and the last time I spoke with her she was being followed by a psychiatrist-finally.

PATIENTS TAUGHT ME

Estella Moore

I arrived at Grady's door very full of myself, as my mother would say. Atlanta was my sole experience with the South. I had an Ivy League education and worked at some rather prestigious institutions in the North. Now, here I was ready to give my skill and expertise to my people and my community at the county hospital. I delivered my resume to Grady in person and was offered an interview on the same day with the Social Service Director, Charlene Turner. The interview went well, I thought. I knew they were impressed with me; after all, I got an interview right away. As the interview ended, I turned to the director and said something like "Charlene, thank you for seeing me." She quickly corrected me, responding that she was Ms. Turner, and had not given me permission to call her by her first name. Wow, welcome to the South.

I soon eased into comfort with Ms. Turner's direct style. Obviously, I needed it. I came to appreciate it and found it quite endearing to have someone you could always count on to tell you the truth about yourself and keep you humble.

I was hired with all direct speed and started as the orthopedic social worker. I remember my first indigent patient with a broken limb needing a ride home. I went to James Reed, my supervisor to get information on department resources. How do I arrange to get a patient home? Does the department use a cab voucher system or what? James told me to call a local funeral home. He said it with a straight face. I thought he didn't understand; my patient is alive! Yes, the department had an arrangement with a few local funeral homes to transport our indigent non-emergent patients. This was before non-emergency transportation vans. I was very unsettled about calling a funeral home to arrange transportation for a live patient, but soon found it was my hang-up, not the patients'. This was the first of many eye-openers at Grady. It was the

Grady Social Service way, in the absence of a way, make a way. In the absence of a resource, create something. While it threw me for a loop at first, I was soon able to adapt.

William Glasser, Harriett Bartlett, William Ryan to name a few, were my select hallmark theoreticians and practitioners learned in social work school, that I had chosen to ingrain in my thinking. They greatly influenced my social work practice and my life, as did the problem-solving emphasis of my social work school. I had gone to a social work school that emphasized and continuously distinguished itself as problem-solving, not psychotherapeutic or functional-based.

I found the many case situations at Grady drew on everything I had and much, much more. I was thankful for the problem-solving background. Grady made you dig deep, as you were exposed to the problems in people's lives. People who had few resources to bring to bear and, as the social worker, you had precious little, as well. But, the patients counted on you and easily gave you their trust. Your tools included advocacy, empowering the patient, empathy, encouraging, teaching, and sometimes just caring and being the listening ear. "The General" as I came to affectionately and respectfully refer to Charlene Turner, shaped a department that institutionalized her leadership qualities. She required professionalism yes, but also, flexibility, openness, smarts, and most of all compassion. "Keep your focus on the patient and give them your best."

Well, a decade later, under "The General's" tutelage, I became the social work supervisor for OB/GYN, or as we familiarly called it "Mother Baby." Among our many responsibilities were supporting mothers through miscarriages and stillbirths, being their advocate, support, and resource through domestic violence situations, supporting them through diagnosis of cancer and HIV/AIDs, helping families to face and deal with cases of incest and sexual assault, etc. We also had to assess and "clear" mothers who tested positive for substances at delivery. We had the challenging task of meeting with substance-abusing mothers at the bedside and confronting them with their positive drug screen. It was challenging, not only because we had to confront the issue, but also because we had to more or less conduct a forensic interview for the report we were mandated to make to the Department of Family and Children Services (DFACS) and the police.

I insisted that workers be honest with our mothers, explaining to them our reporting requirements to DFACS. We let them know DFACS would follow up with them and decide if their baby would go home with them. I was fond of saying to staff that they could say almost anything to anybody; the most important thing was how they said it. My mantra to staff was they had a short period to establish a relationship with our mothers, but they had to work to develop rapport, to try to connect with them. They had to artfully balance truth with caring. It was not an easy thing to tell these mothers their baby might not go home with them.

I remember one day being paged to the office for an emergency. One of my workers had broken "the news" to a mother who was residing in a private drug rehab program. The mother did not take the news well that her baby wasn't being discharged to her. She called the proprietor of the home where she was staying. The proprietor arrived on the mother-baby floor and was very loud and disruptive. I was beeped to the area and told that the proprietor was demanding to see the supervisor—me. I arrived on the floor after racing up eleven flights. (Not that Grady didn't have elevators. There were 4 huge elevators at each end of the corridor. But, there were usually throngs of people getting on and off. If you had to get there quickly, you took the stairs). Arriving on the floor, I went immediately to the office. I wanted to hear an account of the situation from the social worker first hand. To my surprise, I couldn't get into the office. It was not only locked, but a chair or something was propped up against the door.

Thankfully, we had a peephole, and the all-female social work staff that was huddled inside, let me in. Not long after I got in, we all heard my name booming in the hall as I was invited to "Get the hell out here, so I can kick you're a_ _." Yes, I did go out to talk with her, but only after hospital security arrived. I was hoping to live to go home to my family that night.

On my way into work one morning, at the bottom landing of the grand marble staircase that flanked both sides of the main lobby in the hospital, a young man jubilantly greeted me and called me by name. I had no idea who he was, but at least he was happy. He recounted for me that he was my patient from almost a decade earlier. He thanked me and recounted his story.

Following a tragic accident, he needed emergency life-saving surgery. His parents had adamantly opposed the necessary surgical interventions. There was no doubt that they loved him, but on religious grounds, they were staunchly against the surgical interventions. In private, he voiced that he wanted the surgeries. While with his parents he was allowed to save face and voice opposition to surgery. The Grady team swiftly took the case to a judge and got an emergency order allowing us to proceed with the surgery. While in retrospect, the case could have had other outcomes, here he was almost a decade later exuberant about his life. Sadly, I did not know the young man when I saw him and was taken aback that he remembered me.

I am certain that those of us who became social workers are social workers because we love people and because we desire to make their lives better. In doing what we do, our patients make us better. I fondly remember a mother I worked with whose child had sickle cell. Did I mention that "The General" required flexibility? I worked orthopedics, cardiology, sickle cell, neurology, and other areas before going to Mother Baby.

This mother, whose child had Sickle Cell, loved her daughter dearly. At nine years old, the little girl was still being wheeled in a stroller. She had seizures almost daily and took over 90 pills every day. The staff didn't know what to make of the mother, because she read the New England Journal of Medicine like others read a glamor magazine. She knew of every cutting-edge treatment and her knowledge and questions continually challenged the medical staff. She wanted treatments that would fix her daughter and why couldn't she have them. Sadly, her daughter, her only child died. Many years later, she must have moved into the same neighborhood as me. We would run into each other almost weekly at the store. Good outcome, after her period of grief she had gone to nursing school and become a registered nurse.

Thanksgiving. I was paged to the office and found one of my worker's on the phone with an expectant mother who was expressing suicidal ideation. The worker was stuck, exhausted, spent. Understandably, we moved from one case right into another back to back and the cases were emotionally draining. I took over the phone call and the patient shared that she was not only thinking about suicide. She had a plan and was ready to act on it. We continued to talk because my task was to keep her on the phone, communicate my caring, get her to trust me, and join me in believing she had something to live for. Once I was able to get her to tell me where she was, I wrote the address and instructed staff to dispatch the police to her location.

Thankfully, the police got there in time. Much later, the patient came to meet me. Every year after, she came and brought me an updated picture of her little boy the week of Thanksgiving. Over three decades later, working at another hospital, I answered the phone to hear a patient say she was fearful of having an upcoming surgery and her doctor told her to call and talk with his social worker. My caller said, "I know this voice. Can this really be you? "My patient recounted times of my sitting by her bedside at Grady thirty years ago. Her story was that she had been transferred to Grady from her hometown several hours away. She had little or no family and few visitors through a long protracted hospitalization. To my surprise, she described in full detail my various efforts that in some way helped her. She credited me with advocacy efforts that allowed her baby to remain with her for a period so they could bond, help to get her baby supplies, resources, and discharge efforts, etc.

The bottom line — we see many patients and we cannot remember them all. They, however, see only one of us. And, they remember our efforts sharply. Well, here we were on the phone so many years later, a different hospital and she was facing yet another health challenge. We talked through her current challenge, her fears of another long protracted hospitalization, her fears of a bad outcome, her need for this procedure, and then all the possibilities of a good outcome.

When she did come for her procedure, I went to see her as she was being prepped. She introduced me to the staff prepping her as her "friend social worker." Heart-warming. Yes, we give. And yes, at the patient's hand we receive — the opportunity of service, the opportunity to meet a need. Thanks to all my patients for the opportunity to serve.

IT ALL

HAPPENS IN THE ER

GRADY MEMORIES, THE ER, AND THE OLYMPICS

James Reed

My journey at Grady Hospital began in the spring of 1977 with the pursuit to find employment in my chosen field. Coming up to the completion of my MSW and graduation from UGA's MSW program I explored many job opportunities.

I was a new graduate, had received my degree and was looking to have an impact on the world. I was one of the army of young African Americans being challenged to have an impact on society and to better serve the Black community. Several of my contacts at my school as well as close friends had suggested several potential spots to land. Because of my interests, juvenile justice, youth corrections agencies, child welfare agencies and healthcare facilities were suggested as potential employment opportunities. Among the agencies contacted were two highly respected social work programs in the Atlanta community. They included Travelers Aid of Metropolitan Atlanta and Grady Hospital's Social Work Department.

I conducted my research, interviewed at both, and later found myself employed as a social worker at Travelers Aid of Metro Atlanta (TAMA). Though not being offered a position at Grady was somewhat disappointing, I was impressed by its social work leadership and vision. Over the coming months, I would find myself collaborating with Grady's Social Work Department concerning mutual TAMA /Grady cases. This later led to acceptance of a job offer as a medical social worker in the Cardiac Clinic at Grady Hospital.

Employment at Grady would prove to be the start of a wonderful and exciting chapter in my life, which would last over three decades. It would open my eyes to how access or the lack of access to healthcare plays a big part in economic and societal challenges experienced by many of this nation's disenfranchised.

The need for professionally prepared, as well as, culturally sensitive social workers became evident. On a day-to-day basis, I saw many patients, clients and families whose health and lifestyles were compromised due to issues frequently outside of themselves; issues they had no control over. But, through the efforts of excellent social work practitioners, their lives were improved. Travelers Aid of Metropolitan Atlanta had definitely helped to prepare me for the years I would spend at Grady Hospital. It helped me to become more comfortable and self-sufficient in working with those with the least resources and assisted in the development of community contacts.

In looking back over my years at Grady, I can recall so many moving and touching events. Many involved my interactions and activities with other social workers as we supported patient needs and others were instances of mutual support and growth among colleagues. This is the highlight of my Grady years - the wonderful staff and patients I came in contact with regularly and the variety of challenging and interesting cases requiring social work intervention.

The social work department was blessed and led by an outstanding social work administrator named Charlene Turner better known as "CT" or "Ms. T" by her staff. Mrs. Turner is considered a social worker's social worker, open to getting her hands dirty and willing to go beyond the call of duty. She is characterized by having a good sense of humor and a passion for life. Above all else, she is known for challenging her social work team to advocate for meeting the needs of patients and families and also to educate and motivate other hospital staff in a similar manner.

While serving as a social worker I was regularly called upon to rise above the call of duty for patients. Some of the most unusual cases occurred during my time as an ER social worker and later as the supervisor for the ER social work team. Several of these instances highlight the challenge as well as the commitment to excellence exhibited by social work staff. Let me first acknowledge, Grady's Emergency Room is like no other ER in the metro Atlanta area; it is typically staffed by individuals that manage excitement and trauma effectively and some might even describe them as adrenaline junkies.

One good case example involves a patient identified as Ms. G who had been referred to the social work team by the emergency room staff. This particular referral was to provide assistance to a female patient presenting to the ER because of chronic seizure problems and homelessness. On this occasion, social work staff was called upon to assist this patient with obtaining needed seizure medications, locating stable housing and obtaining dry clothing for discharge. (Unfortunately, the patient had soiled her clothing during her seizure).

While interviewing the patient on this date and during future visits to the hospital; I learned that she suffered from an Intellectual disability and had been hospitalized in a state facility at an early age in her life. She remained a ward of the state until becoming a young adult and later found herself wandering from place to place in the metro area. Though encumbered with a disability she found a way to have joy in her life and developed positive relationships with many of the hospital staff as well as individuals in the community. This particular patient became a regular in the ER and even became well known to the administrative team often accessing their offices more easily than some of the physicians. I and several other departmental social workers became constants in her life; working with her on medication management, housing support and developing a strong social network. Informally we became her family and supported her need for independence. She pushed back on any effort for permanent placement. All placements failed within a short period of time; she would move into a stable home for a brief period but return to Grady within days of this disposition. We even attempted to get her signed on as a hospital volunteer and this worked somewhat, as she was assigned to the social services and the chaplaincy department. This was an effective idea because she loved the hospital, its staff, and we were perceived as her family and social support system.

As a volunteer she was helpful and could be depended upon to assist with locating clothing for patients in need. This was indeed her specialty and somewhat understandable in that staff had to always find clothing for Ms. G when she presented to the ER for seizures with her clothing soiled by urine.

I can remember on one occasion she was found stuck under a pile of clothing in the clothing closet. This was when we knew we needed to take back the clothing closet key because she was going through the closet without being requested. Ms. G was a fixture for years in the Grady community and gave all of her favorite social workers a nickname. As the years passed and her health deteriorated, a decision had to finally be made to place her in a nursing home facility. I along with other members of the social work team struggled with this decision but adhered and located a facility out of town. She passed within the next year and a memorial service was held at a local church in Decatur, GA. I and several members of Grady's ER and social services team were present. We all spoke at the service about our love for her and how we witnessed her need to be independent. We acknowledged her as an individual who though diagnosed with a disability had her own level of independence. She could be seen working at the Atlanta Braves' games selling hot dogs, working as a volunteer in the hospital, and just being the unique person she was. I am proud of the respect shown to this patient by the hospital and social services staff making the effort to provide creative support to the most needy.

During my time of providing social work coverage in the ER, the multi-disciplinary partnership was exceptional; it was a time when physicians, nurses and social workers took on any problem and worked toward a positive solution. One such challenging situation arose during this period, when early one morning in the old Surgical Emergency Clinic (SEC) social work was consulted and requested to meet with a patient refusing medical care. *(Dr. Gail Anderson and Dr. Daniel Golightly were the lead physicians at that time and they both were dedicated to social work excellence and producing positive outcomes with patient care).*

The medical team informed me they had a male patient requiring a below the knee amputation to save his life. He had already been approached by several members of the surgery team but refused consent for the procedure. Following review of the case with his physicians and nurses I entered his room and found a middle-aged Black couple. The male patient was lying on a stretcher with a female sitting in a chair nearby. I approached the patient and introduced myself, asking if we could speak. He agreed. Patient confidentiality guidelines and privacy concerns were discussed. He identified the female guest as his fiancé and requested that she stay for any discussion. He spoke about his health and his desire to be married before he lost his leg to amputation. He felt that he would not be a whole man if he did not have his leg for their upcoming marriage. His fiancé was supportive and affirmed her love throughout the discussion. She told him the leg had nothing to do with their love but he still had difficulty with shifting his mindset.

Following this interview, I discussed the barriers to surgery with the clinical team and exploring the possibility of having the couple married in the ER prior to surgery. The team was on board with this idea and it was presented to the patient and his fiancé. They both were excited and in agreement; details were discussed on how to pull this off within several hours. The idea was presented to necessary hospital entities (hospital administration, social work administration, public relations, and legal affairs) to insure compliance. With this last hurdle completed, the hard work started; how to get this wedding performed within several hours and get Mr. G into surgery.

Chaplaincy was contacted and the ER Chaplain agreed to perform the ceremony; contact was made with staff in the marriage license office located in the Fulton County Health Department building adjacent to the hospital. They identified the steps needed for a valid marriage license (lab work, signatures and other information). Nurses in the ER drew blood for the couple and expedited it through the labs, ER Registration assisted with completion of paperwork, Public Relations assisted with flowers from the hospital's gift shop and photography from their staff for the ceremony. This was indeed a miraculous undertaking but with the support of social work and other hospital colleagues we would make this happen. This process started early that morning around 9:00am and shortly after lunch the ceremony was being performed in the ER. It was a wonderful wedding with great support provided by the hospital's team. Regrettably, the reception had to be cut out as this patient had surgery scheduled.

The surgical procedure was successful and this marriage was started off by being showered with the love and support provided by Grady Social Work and Grady's Emergency Room staff. I couldn't linger long with the family following the wedding because other social work consults had to be answered but this was truly an amazing day and wedding in the Grady ER.

Addendum:
Before the wedding could take place, Charlene had to convince one of the administrators over the ER that this was appropriate. The administrator felt that this was not appropriate for the ER and the use of a treatment room. Upon hearing this, Ms. Turner headed straight to her office and in her "Chicago style" of advocacy, remained standing and boldly proceeded to tell her why this wedding needed to happen. After submitting this case to her for the book, Ms. Turner reflected with that Charlene Turner smile, "I'm not sure I adhered to good social work principles." Ms. Turner got the needed approval and joined us in the ER to observe the ceremony. She complimented us on garnering multi-

disciplinary involvement and the nursing staff who had even decorated the IV pole and the entire treatment room. This case actually has a second happy ending. Years later, Mr. G appeared in the social service office and expressed his gratitude. He told us he was still happily married.

Another memorable time in the ER occurred during the summer of 1996. This was an exciting time for the state of Georgia and especially the metro Atlanta area. The state was excited at the idea of hosting the Summer Olympics. Grady Hospital was gearing up to support healthcare needs for the many visitors expected in the downtown area. Social workers and the Social Work Department spruced up its guidelines for service delivery. Key departments met as an Olympics Task Force within the hospital and within the broader community to review protocols, update resources, troubleshoot operations to best serve the additional volume of expected patients and guests. Hospital staff modified their coverage guidelines by staggering shift times to meet the increased volume of traffic on the city streets and highways. We were a very proud and excited group of individuals.

The Olympics Task Force resulted in the social service department strengthening its trauma response practices. As social service answered to the Department of Medical Affairs at that time, there was a strong connection between social workers and physicians which allowed for the Social Service Department to have the necessary resources to meet any challenge that might arrive. This connection was critical in allowing the department to implement 24/7 coverage staffing in the ER with MSW's and social work assistants assigned to each shift. The strength of this model as well as the teams' rapid response would be shown to pay dividends and resulted in an improved response to social work challenges requiring intervention. Team members in the years coming up to the Olympics responded to high risk referrals such as (motor vehicle collisions, gunshot wounds, interpersonal violence injuries, child abuse referrals, industrial accidents, sudden deaths, and other traumatic injuries). They collaborated closely with ER staff (physicians, nurses, etc.), and key Grady Departments such as Chaplaincy,

Psychiatry, Food Service, Emergency Medical Services, and Security), as well as partnering with local Law Enforcement, the local Department of Family and Children Services and other community agencies.

On the morning of July 27, 1996 the many months of preparation and preparedness would be tested. At 1: 20 AM a pipe bomb exploded in the Centennial Olympic Park causing 1 fatality and injuries to 111 individuals. This explosion was the act of a domestic terrorist and threw shockwaves throughout the community. A call was made to Grady Hospital and all trauma responders were alerted. The disaster (Code D) Plan for Grady Hospital Social Workers went live. The call made its cycle through the telephone tree and all key personnel were alerted. Twenty plus social work staff responded to the call. Chaplaincy was notified, outpatient psychiatry representatives were contacted and other key service providers were notified.

Social work staff responded and reported to their assigned areas. Day (1st shift) and evening (2nd shift) ER social workers rushed in and provided support and assistance to the night (3rd shift) ER social worker team in the ER. ER social workers collected background information and details on patients, notifying their family members and providing the needed crisis intervention support required for this traumatic event. Other Social work staff members reported to the ground floor auditorium which had been turned into a receiving (waiting room) area for family members and friends seeking information on patients that may have been injured. The main office of Social Services became the Central Command location for all social work operations. Our front desk was staffed and received incoming calls from family, friends, news media outlets, and others in the local community. Critical information was relayed to medical affairs leadership, keeping them apprised and insuring that pertinent information was conveyed to the Executive Team. The entire social work leadership team was available and responded as needed to the challenge. Implementation of a trauma alert system for social services was working and successful. We had drilled this process over the months coming up to the Olympics and conducted several test runs to ensure awareness. As social workers at the largest public hospital in the state of Georgia, we knew the pressure was on us and the community was looking to us to answer the call.

The responsiveness by the social work team on this date was one of the department's proudest moments at Grady. All social work staff came together, regardless of their assigned coverage areas, to meet the needs of this trauma. Some staff arrived within an hour of the event; others arrived several hours later to provide relief and support to colleagues and then others reported in the afternoon to assist with 2nd shift needs. The effort was outstanding and allowed for the most critical to be served first and allowed for few to be neglected. The team worked closely throughout this weekend ensuring the hospital had met the needs of the many visitors seeking medical care at Grady due to the Olympic Park Bombing.

As days passed and Olympic activities resumed, the social work team knew it had earned a gold medal for its response to one of the city's most traumatic events. We would not receive notice in the press nor on news stations but we knew we had accomplished something special by the services provided to those affected by the Olympic Park Bombing.

This is just one example of the kind of work Mr. Reed did in the ER as a staff social worker and later when he supervised the workers in that area.
Charlene Turner

KNOWING THE DEATH SCRIPT ALL TOO WELL

Claudia Taylor

Working in a Level One Trauma Center emergency room as a social worker you never know who or what you may encounter on a daily basis. Car accidents, gunshot wounds, falls, stabs and burns are only a few of the situations you are called to assist with-to reach out and provide support to families as they learn of the conditions of the patient. For me, each trauma produced somewhat of an adrenaline rush. I got used to seeing the blood, open wounds, exposed bones, and even a heart. It didn't rattle or unnerve me. It gave me a glimpse of what the body looks like on the inside in real life instead of what's on the movie screens.

Once I learned the condition of the patient, as the social worker, I was the one to determine the legal next of kin, make the call, and inform them of the condition of the patient. In making the call the question becomes what script am I going to use in an effort to try and keep the family calm and not try to answer those questions that are out of the scope of social work. Will they live, what kind of surgery are they having, what's their prognosis?

One of the most difficult experiences in reaching out to a family to notify them of their loved one's presence at the hospital is knowing someone is deceased at the time of the call and being unable to divulge that information. Almost every time I picked up the telephone to say your loved one is here at Grady, are you available to come, the question was always, well how are they? This was a question I really did not want to respond to because I know my response caused me to paint a picture of some hope that the deceased is alive. My heart was racing during the call because I must not lie but I have to say something so I use the script; "they are in critical condition and once you get here the doctors will give you more information".

Gratefully that line prevented further questioning and soon I would have to see these family members face to face. In meeting them, there is a part of me that aches because I somewhat feel as though my friendliness and my half-smile relays a message that their family member will be alright with breath still in their body but the reality which they will soon learn, is death.

Being a part of a support team in the notification of someone's death was filled with emotion because I had to figure out how to hold back the tears as I stood and heard a mother's cry, watched a husband punch the wall, and or saw a child pass out on the floor once learning of the death. Most of the time, I ask God to help me be strong and find the right words to say before we (chaplain, and doctor) enter the family waiting room for this delivery because someone has lost a part of their family unexpectedly. I have to endure the moment as the doctor says their script to the person who received the call from me the social worker. "Ok tell me what you know happened? …. OK, yes your loved one came in with a gunshot wound to the chest. When paramedics arrived they administered CPR and upon their arrival to Grady, we continued CPR for three minutes but unfortunately, we could not save them".

The facial expressions, the screams, and the cries are piercing to my soul and I must get myself together to continue providing support to this family because the physician has left the room, and tells the family to let the social worker know if there are any additional questions and they will try to answer them if available. Now I am left with the family to express condolences, but I also want to say, "I am sorry. Sorry, if I gave you all an inch of hope that your family member was alive knowing they were deceased from the moment I first said hello and you answered." It's so interesting that the same script I was so familiar with, my script as well as the doctor's, seemed to be one that was also written at another hospital. Déjà vu … eerie, interesting…

When my best friend passed away in 2014, someone at the hospital called her mother to say my BFF was found down. She was in critical condition and upon arrival to the hospital, more information would be given by the doctor. From the time we gathered in that family room and the doctor faced her mother and asked, " tell me what you know happened?" I knew she was gone as it was the same script that I knew all too well. It is a script that I wish did not have to be said by doctors to parents, to children, to spouses, to grandparents, and even friends. And, it's a role co-starring the social worker that I wish didn't include us, but it is reality and not what's just on a movie screen.

THE RIGHT OF CHOICE

Venita Griffin Brown

As an Emergency Room Social Worker at Grady Hospital, I have worked with many patients, whose presenting problems were all variants of traumatic life experiences. Social workers are trained to respect patient's rights and their decisions of choice, unbiased by what decisions we would make on their behalf, or what we feel is in their best interest concerning their personal situations.

I remember a young 28-year-old black male who was transported to the emergency room by ambulance in very critical condition. He was conscious, but he had been shot multiple times, mostly in the trunk and abdomen areas of his body. His ER Nurse requested my presence within 10-15 minutes of his admission to the emergency room. His nurse reported she needed my intervention to direct her and the ER security officer as to what they should do. They had discovered that the patient had between $20,000.00 to 25,000.00 on his person that needed to be secured in Patient Belongings. The nurse went on to say that it looked like the patient would not survive for very long, he was bleeding out, and surgery would not likely help him. I met individually with the patient to determine his legal next of kin. He was not married, had no children, and did not know his father. I got his mother's basic information and learned that she lived locally in the city.

My patient told me he lived with his girlfriend, who he said he loved a lot. Of his own initiative, he told me that he had a lot of money on him. He went on to say, if he should die, he wanted his girlfriend to have all of his money. He gave me his girlfriend's name, her date of birth, their address, and her telephone number. I quickly typed a draft of his statement that his money, on his person when he arrived in the Emergency Room, be released in its entirety to his girlfriend should he die. He signed it and his ER Nurse and our Hospital Security Officer witnessed his signature. Sadly, he died approximately 30 minutes after he signed this affidavit.

His girlfriend arrived in the Emergency Room after he expired. Her identity was established, and his ER physician met with her, explained what had transpired with the patient and that he had died. We explained to her that the patient told us both verbally and in writing that she was to receive the entire sum of his money, if he should die.

During this transaction, the patient's mother arrived at the ER, very frantic, and she was told by the patient's ER physician that he had expired. His mother immediately inquired about the patient's belongings and wanted to retrieve what was put in his property. She was told that her son's belongings were released to his girlfriend at his request. The patient's mother went on to report that she was aware that her son was a "dope dealer", and he always had a lot of money on him at any given time. She demanded that I be fired. She insisted that as the social worker, I should not have allowed her son's money to be released to his girlfriend. Her argument was that her son "was not in a right state of mind, not speaking from a sane mind," that he "had been shot all up." She went on, "He was not in his right mind to make any decision, especially about who should get his money."

Of course, I had to undergo an investigative inquiry by my social work supervisors, and with the heads of Security and Legal Affairs. Because I recorded the patient's statement to me and I read the statement back to him before he signed it and it was also witnessed by his ER Nurse and Security,

It was treated as an Affidavit. The patient's mother had no legal leg to stand on. The ER treating physician substantiated also that of the patient's many, many wounds, he had no head trauma, he was not cognitively impaired, and he remained conscious for a good 30 minutes in the ER. My patient had also verbalized to his physician that he knew he probably would not make it and that he would die. This was right before he flatlined. He was pronounced dead within an hour of his arrival in the ER.

As social workers, we have to stand on our integrity. We have to have the courage to protect the patient's right to individual choice and decision-making, irrespective of what their family members feel should happen, or in this case, should not have happened.

CODE TRIAGE

Sandra Sanders

Charge Nurse, Charge Resident, and Attending is the way that most traumatic or medical emergency calls begin. When hearing, "Charge Nurse, Charge Resident, and Attending" you often become more alert, more aware to hear what trauma or medical emergency is to follow: gunshot wound (GSW), stabbing, motor vehicle collision (MVC), burns, falls, cardiovascular accident (CVA) or cardiac arrest. On this Friday morning in March 2007 what was to follow the three charging entities was **CODE TRIAGE**, which is the alert for mass casualty. Grady Health System often prepares staff for a mass casualty incident, with drills and annual training, but you realize when it is occurring in real-time, you have to be prepared for the unexpected.

The social worker's responsibility when hearing the opening of a major notification is to be prepared to interact with patients, families, and be a liaison between families and staff. The social worker in the Grady Health System Emergency Care Center (ECC), must provide a calming demeanor so that those around you remain calm during a traumatic or medical emergency ordeal. One must practice active listening skills for all interactions that occur in the ECC, that's in case you have to testify. The social worker must be able to take action at a fast pace and hectic setting that is often associated with traumas and medical emergencies.

The three major skill sets that the social worker must have when working in the ECC is: communication, critical thinking, and empathy. On that Friday, in March 2007 the three listed characteristics were put to the test for the social workers and social work administrators at Grady Hospital. The social worker must be able to communicate with people from all walks of life, as the ECC, serves a diverse patient population. The social worker must be able to communicate effectively and efficiently, so that the patient and families have a clear understanding of what is occurring, and what the social worker will be able to provide, within one's scope of practice. The social workers in the ECC utilize their skill set to notify families that their family member is at Grady, and to be a liaison between families and medical providers.

Critical thinking is the next proficiency that is important in working in a fast-paced ECC. "Critical thinking is the ability to analyze information gathered from unbiased observation and communication." The social worker must be able to analyze, prioritize, make quick decisions, and formulate the best plan to assist the patient and their family members. [1]

The third most important skill is Empathy. NASW defines it as "the act of perceiving, understanding, experiencing, and responding to the emotional state and ideas of another person." Grady's ECC is a level one trauma center that deals with a lot of hurt, pain, and loss, one must be able to empathize with patients and families that present to the emergency clinic.[2]

On that Friday morning, March 2007 Grady Triage was notified of a mass casualty. A bus carrying a baseball team had plunged off a highway ramp and slammed onto the 1-75 highway below. Grady was immediately notified that it would receive mass causalities. In hearing the call, I took seconds to process. I realize that I had to utilize my critical thinking skills and develop a plan to make immediate notification. I immediately contacted Social Worker Administrators, because I understood that it would be the responsibility of Social Services to contact families, provide support, and provide empathy to the families that were not there with their loved ones. An additional responsibility would be to provide as much information to mothers and fathers of the youth that were involved in the bus crash.

As the first patient presented to the triage area, I remember the strong smell of gasoline in the air and the feelings of anxiousness that surrounded me. The medical staff worked diligently to get vital signs and assess injuries. My thought was to get names and contact phone numbers for the patients' families. I went to work, assisting in identifying patients, and obtaining emergency contact phone numbers. I would go back to the office and contact mothers and fathers, to advise that their child was in the Grady Health System's ECC. For many of the mothers and fathers, who lived in another state, I could hear the fear in their voices, as they had gotten word of the bus crash.

With each patient and each family that I contacted, although there was some level of relief, I understood that they needed to put eyes on their child. The fear, the uncertainty of the relatives, was in large part due to not receiving definitive information on the injuries the patient had incurred. With each call, it felt as if the parents were holding their breath in anticipation of that phone call that their child was alright, and then you could sense the exhale. But, there was a concern that you could hear in the voices of the parents not knowing if the patient had broken bones, head injuries, or any debilitating wound/damage that could impact the rest of his life.

I remember not having time to process what had happened, just taking the time to utilize those three important skills, communication, critical thinking, and empathy. Ensuring that one remains calm, provides support, and empathizes with the patients and their families through these very difficult situations can sometimes be challenging, but always an absolute necessity. As is always the case, these patients were scared. Their families were many miles away, not able to immediately present to the emergency room, most would have to get on a plane and travel to Atlanta. As the day shift staff transitioned in, Social Services administration presented to the ECC, the social work office of the

Grady Health System ECC became the Hub. The Hub was the area where calls were filtered, from family, friends, media, and volunteers. The Hub was the place where people were directed to offer housing for families and give donations to assist families and patients. The Hub was the place where the social worker would make calls to see where the victims of the bus crash were taken if they were not at Grady. The Hub was the place where the social worker would provide that support and empathy to families once they arrived in Atlanta. The Hub was the heart of such a horrific tragedy.

On that Friday in March when I left Grady Health System's ECC, I allowed myself to exhale. I had not realized, but I too was holding my breath, not in anticipation of anything, but in not allowing myself to feel the sadness of what had occurred. While I was in my car, I could still smell the gasoline, I could still feel the anxiousness, and I had to pull over, because I was so sick to my stomach, and I had to purge. I realized at that movement, I needed to allow myself to release the uneasiness, and the grief that I was feeling for the people who had lost their lives, and had been seriously injured in the crash, and their families.

Years later I ask myself, what did I learn, what did I see, what did I come to understand? I learned that the lessons and social work principles I was taught as a Grady Social Worker will be useful for whatever path I choose to take in my social work career. I learned that when something traumatic occurs, we come together and work together for the benefit of the patient and their family. Although many patients were assessed and remained in the ECC, others went to various floors, and the social workers in those areas ensured that all needs were met. I learned the importance of a cool head and supportive and knowledgeable leadership.

Very significantly, I learned these three skills are invaluable: communication, critical thinking and empathy.

---

[1] http://socialwork.buffalo.edu/admissions/is-social-work-right-career-for-me/list-of-essential-skills-in-social-work.html

[2] Barker, R. L. (2003). The Social Work Dictionary. 5th ed. Washington, DC: NASW Press.

MEET THE DISASTER JUNKIES

Charlene Turner

If you get an "adrenalin rush" and spring into action when a disaster announcement comes, I suppose that makes you a disaster junkie. This phrase was coined by a colleague who observed (from a distance) how our department responded to such announcements. I am not sure this colleague meant those words in a complimentary fashion —but I took it as such. Let me begin by saying that nowhere in my social work training did I learn the elements of social work intervention in disasters. We were taught about problem-solving and maneuvering in crises -and combined with "trial and error, we developed a workable protocol for our disaster work at the hospital.

Early in my job as director (1980), Atlanta had what was termed as the Bowen Homes Explosion. Shortly after arriving at work —the news came that there had been a major explosion at a daycare center and the injured were coming to Grady. We later learned that several children and one teacher had been killed. All victims were transported to the hospital and our department became the central spot for families to assemble. There was mass confusion about the injured and who might have died —but the news was out—and families rushed to the hospital in huge numbers. Many parents had rushed to the scene —could not locate their child and then came to the hospital (later we discovered that some of the children were picked up by other relatives and cell phones were not in use at the time). The many families wanted answers about the status of their child —but communication in the midst of treating the injured and getting the deceased to the morgue took hours — and these families became more desperate with each passing moment.

Any family members arriving at the hospital were directed to Social Service and our waiting room became crowded and almost chaotic as the hours passed. I was forced to make some quick decisions —so

I decided to group each family with two social workers (by this time we knew we had five families) —and each family had seven or eight people. The social workers then took each family into an individual office to "wait" for more information. It took some time to determine which children were in the morgue and we had to be certain before families were informed —each family desperately wanted answers. We came to the point of describing the clothing each "missing" child had worn to the center that day —and then matching those descriptions with the morgue. These families began to plead for answers —and even when we had the answers, I had a senior administrator advising me not to tell them. I kept insisting that I had to inform these families —and after some tense moments in our conversation —he finally relented.

Once we informed the parents, each family was insistent about going to the morgue. Of course, the morgue was telling us to not let the families come—again we had to let the morgue know that they were coming and that they needed to somehow get the children ready for viewing. The assigned social workers then had to accompany their family to the morgue and try to offer as much support as possible. I will now acknowledge that the staff assigned to work with these families was not a random choice —but I called on those who had demonstrated leadership, the ability to "think clearly" in the midst of crises, and to proceed with compassion above all else. I should add that this explosion took place at a time when tension in Atlanta was high due to the Missing and Murdered Children episode in the city —and there was speculation from many community leaders that this was a malicious act aimed at killing more black children.

Needless to say, this was probably the most difficult experience in my career. At the end of the day, I felt like someone had punched me in the stomach —I was so weak I could barely make it to my car. I had experienced the overwhelming grief of these families (my own children were the same age as these children) and was left with the question of whether we had done enough. We had invited chaplaincy to participate —but social work took the lead in dealing with each family. At that time, we had no disaster protocol for the department-but one was quickly developed and we were now "on ready."

There were several other disaster calls over the years (a courthouse shooting with several victims, the Buckhead Shooting, the Ohio Bus crash, etc.), but the one that stayed in my mind the most was the Olympic Park Bombing. We were so ready for this event (or so we thought) as much planning had been done in preparation for Atlanta's time in the limelight. We had meetings with city officials and the police department to discuss strategy in case of a bad occurrence. By this time, our department had "perfected" a disaster protocol with a detailed plan of action. Our major role was to work with families and keep them informed of the status of the injured. In essence, we dealt with the anxiety and fear of the families, regardless of the outcome. We became the message carriers for the medical staff and assisted them whenever there was a need to deliver "bad news" to families.

I received a call in the early am about a bombing in Centennial Park – telling me to report to the hospital. We had a telephone "notification" tree –and I was to call whoever was next in line. Somehow, I thought I was dreaming and turned over to go back to sleep. A few minutes later, I received a second call—then I knew it was real. I hurriedly got dressed and hit I-20 doing 80-or 90 miles an hour –so disappointed that I did not respond to the first call.
I rushed to the Grady Auditorium which was the designated spot for families to assemble and there I was met by our nighttime social work assistant. I will never forget his words – "Ms. Turner, I am glad to see you –but you cannot embarrass the department in those mismatched shoes." Luckily, I had a spare pair in the office and quickly retreated to change shoes. We were so well prepared that I essentially just stood by and watched as the ER social workers took charge.

Our department was later commended for the work we did that night. All of us worked overtime that night as the adrenalin was definitely flowing. Two developments caught us by surprise—the intervention of the FBI was one, as they stepped in and told the rest of us that they were in charge. Also, we had not taken into consideration the time changes and the language difficulties when the rest of the world woke up to the news of a bombing —so we had to make some immediate adjustments to accommodate these new calls from around the world.

I cannot emphasize enough the "disaster action plan" we developed over time. Kudos go to James Reed, our ER supervisor at the time, for his outstanding leadership during most of the disasters. He even kept a "disaster kit" under his desk that contained the protocol he outlined for us to follow in such crises. By the time of the Olympics, Mr. Reed and his team were so adept at what we needed to do that I mainly became a bystander and just followed their orders.

EMERGENCY ROOM MEMORIES

Dorothy F. Carrillo

Grady Hospital and its emergency room have always been incredible places to work. As a social worker, you are challenged, gratified, outraged, and sometimes overwhelmed. On a macro level, you see the enormity of poverty and the resulting social problems. You see the effects of racism "up close and personal". On a micro level, you serve people who are proud, hardworking and doing their best to survive. You also meet people who have been devastated by life or their limitations and have turned to addiction, crime, and abuse of others.

In 1970, the Grady Hospital Emergency Room was in fact, two facilities separated by a wide hallway. If you entered from the ambulance ramp which at that time was on the southwest side of the hospital, the door on your left was the Surgical ER and the Medical ER was to the right. Originally, like everything else at Grady until the hospital was integrated in 1959, there were two ERs, and a patient's race determined on which side they would receive treatment.

On the wall outside each ER were plaques in honor of Margaret Mitchell, author of "Gone with the Wind". In 1949, while crossing Peachtree Street to attend a movie with her husband, Ms. Mitchell was struck by a passing cab. She was taken by ambulance to the Grady emergency room where she died of her injuries. Given Ms. Mitchell's universal popularity, the pride Atlantans felt for her, and the public mourning over her death, it was fitting at that time to give the ER her name.

Although Ms. Mitchell quietly and anonymously made significant contributions to education for African Americans during her lifetime, it should not be lost on anyone that her great homage to the antebellum south would be the catalyst for honoring her in what was then a segregated institution.

Looking back, I remember everything as green. The hallways, the walls, and the floor tiles of the ER were all different shades of dark to medium green. Despite the lighting, the area was gloomy and appeared to need a good cleaning even after the area had just been cleaned, which happened several times each day.

Entry to the medical side of the ER was through swinging double doors. Once inside you faced a long rectangular room. In the middle of the room against the wall was the long, wooden receiving desk where doctors and nurses updated patients' charts or ordered various tests and procedures. Directly across from the receiving desk was the medicine room. The oversized door to this room was always open since staff were constantly moving in and out of it. Individual treatment rooms were situated to the right and left off the rest of the main room.

I was a medical social worker at Grady Hospital, assigned to the 6th-floor cardiac unit where I assisted patients and their families with discharge planning, economic needs, and emotional issues arising from the family member's illness. I was also assigned to the outpatient medical clinic.

Every five weeks I did double duty and was on-call in the emergency room. My duties were on the medical side and I considered myself lucky. The surgical side was the "bloody" side where incidents like "shot by a friend" were treated. Atlanta was much less populated in those days so most accident and burn victims were brought to the Surgical ER.

When ER staff needed to contact me, they would call the Social Services Department or page me. The loudspeaker system could be heard throughout the hospital and I would hastily conclude whatever I was doing and hurry to the ground floor.

Referrals from the ER were generally about patients with no place to go or someplace to go but no transportation to get there. Also, I was frequently called upon to locate a patient's family with scant information to go on. But more about that later. I would also note that during the three-plus years I worked at Grady, the ER patients I dealt with were all males.

I would approach the receiving desk and the nurse or doctor would tell me what was needed. I would scan the chart before going to talk with the patient. Patients who were ready for discharge but waiting to see the social worker were seated in large wood-framed wheelchairs near the receiving desk. The challenge was to create some privacy for the patient and myself during the interview. To do this I would sit in a chair next to the patient, lean in, and speak in a soft voice that the patient could hear, but not everyone in the ER. I would ask him to describe where he lived and with whom; to tell me about his financial resources; what he did each day; and I would explain the nature of the assistance I could provide for him.

Often, I would contact a family that would refuse to have anything to do with the patient. The family was exhausted from years of dealing with the patient who had abused or taken advantage of them, made promises that were not kept, or was disruptive to the family in some way.

Patients with no place to go and no family available or willing to take them were referred to the Union Mission or the Salvation Army. I would contact the intake person at the facility and discuss the patient's medical and financial situation. If the patient was accepted, I would arrange transportation, often a hospital vehicle. Patients rarely refused and were often grateful to be "off the streets". Only one time do I recall a man refusing services and insisting on leaving the ER on his own. He hated the idea of going to a homeless shelter and preferred the life he knew on the streets.

Another type of referral from the ER included locating relatives when the patient would not give us the information or could not provide enough information. This involved some detective work. I would examine the chart for any clues. Sometimes a previous admission sheet would have some information such as an old address, family member's name, or previous employment. Using the city directory, I could identify if family members lived at an address. I might call the personnel department of a previous employer. One time I called a well-known company and they gave me ten-year-old information that led straight to the patient's sister.

Another time a patient died in the ER with no next-of-kin listed. In fact, the patient had adamantly and loudly refused to give the admitting nurse any information and she noted that on the chart. The patient died and the body lay in the morgue waiting to be claimed. I was able to locate a sister and asked her to come to the hospital regarding her brother. Within an hour five family members arrived. I sat-in while the doctor explained why the patient died.

The family was shocked, hurt, and angry. They blamed the hospital staff for failing to find them before he died. They would not accept that their brother had refused to give us the information to locate them. The emotions in the room were palpable and the pain was evident on the faces of the family. From my social work training, I knew the best action to take in the present moment was no action. I do not know how long I sat and let them pour out their rage, but it seemed like forever.

Finally, I sensed they were talked out. I was then able to talk them through the patient's admission to the ER, showing them on the chart the note regarding his insistence that he had no relatives. Then I gently inquired why they thought he might have made this statement. After a short period of silence, family members began to talk about the tensions within the family and specifically as related to their brother. By the time they were through it was clear why the patient had denied their existence. Their anger turned to immense sadness and they asked to claim the body for burial.

After a few months on the job the ER referrals became routine. However, two not-so-routine incidents standout in my mind. I was leaving the ER and stepped out into the hallway just as the EMTs came through the door from the ambulance ramp pushing a gurney. Under the sheets, you could make out the figure of a patient.

Normally I would not even glance at this out of respect to the patient, but this time the EMT stopped me and said, "You've got to see this". He pulled up the sheet from the foot of the gurney exposing a newborn just minutes old. The umbilical cord was still connected to the mother. He told me how he had delivered the baby in the ambulance on the way to the hospital. He was as proud as if it was his child.

The other incident was completely different. If local police apprehended someone who needed immediate medical attention, they would bring them to the Grady ER. Usually, the arrests were for public drunkenness or disturbing the peace. The policeman would handcuff the person to the arm of a wheelchair. After treatment, these patients were wheeled into the main room of the ER to await arrest.

I had just finished interviewing a patient who needed a place to go. I stood by the receiving desk talking with a nurse. I was oblivious to the man handcuffed to the wheelchair just to my right, and the fact that he had managed to uncuff himself. With lightning speed, he stood up, grabbed my arms, and pulled them around to my back. Then he began to yell, "Don't try to stop me or I'll hurt her. Leave me alone or I'll hurt her." He moved around so I was in front of him while he marched back toward the open door of the medicine room. He must have thought the open door was the exit. Immediately as he crossed the threshold of the medicine room, two ambulance attendants who had been taking a break in that room grabbed him from behind, marched him back to the wheelchair, and tied his hands and feet with restraints.

Someone asked me if I was alright and as soon as I said yes, a feeling of "what could have happened" came over me. My stomach began to churn and my head to reel. I walked over and leaned my back against the wall. My knees gave way and I sank to the ground. The next thing I remember was the smell of ammonia from a vial a nurse had pressed to my nose. How the ambulance attendants saved the social worker became the talk of the hospital. That was my fifteen minutes of fame.

Emergency room duty was a serious responsibility. You would not even consider taking a vacation or sick leave if it was your week in the ER. It was a heavy load for a social worker to cover our inpatient units, outpatient clinics, and the ER. You would never want to ask another social worker to cover for you unless you had a personal emergency and it had better be a big one.

So, having lived in Atlanta most of my life, when the worst ice storm of the century hit the city, I knew the drill: schools close, businesses shut down, and we all stay home. However, emergency services like hospitals, utility repair, snow removal, and law enforcement went on.

Snow days had been wonderful events when I was growing up. Of course, it meant freedom from school. Then we would dress in whatever we had to venture out into the snow. Not normally needing heavy winter clothes, we would concoct odd outfits, layers consisting of a t-shirt, turtleneck, and sweater, several pairs of socks, the warmest coat we could find; odd pairs of gloves and mismatched scarves and hats.

The neighborhood kids would gather on the lawn and begin to build snowmen. A snowball fight would invariably breakout. At some point, we would head for the snow-covered slopes of the Ansley Park Golf Course, dragging along large pieces of cardboard, purloined metal Coca-Cola signs, and even a bona fide sled. Once at the hill the real fun would begin as over and over we slid down that slope on our mostly makeshift sleds.

But, on that February morning, I had ER duty and had to get from my suburban apartment to the downtown hospital. I dressed in what passes for warm clothing in a city that rarely has temperatures below 32 degrees. Outside, my car was covered in ice. The door locks were frozen, and the windshield was caked with the white stuff. I heated my car key with a cigarette lighter and unlocked the door. I made several trips from the apartment to the car carrying hot water to pour on the windshields and used a makeshift scraper to do the rest. Time was passing and I was going to be late.

Once in the car, I turned the ignition, and nothing happened. The battery was dead. Just as panic set in, redemption arrived in the form of a city bus. Before today, I had not noticed there was a bus stop in front of my apartment complex. I flagged the bus down and began the perilous ride downtown to Grady and to ER duty.

So much for the carefree snow days of youth.

EVERYTHING I NEEDED TO KNOW:

BUT DID NOT LEARN IN SOCIAL WORK SCHOOL

CLOSING GRADY'S DIALYSIS CLINIC

Louise M. Spiro

The Grady Dialysis Clinic was the first clinic in Georgia to offer dialysis when not everyone requiring dialysis could receive it. At that time, panels would decide who would best benefit to receive this lifesaving treatment. Everything changed in 1972, when the Federal Government added dialysis to Medicare. This new entitlement required a person to be on dialysis for three months (acute dialysis) before being considered as having a chronic renal disease that required lifetime dialysis (or a transplant) to live. Then an individual could receive Dialysis Medicare as long as he had paid into the system. Dialysis centers opened everywhere. This is important to understand so that one can see what happened to Grady's Dialysis Clinic.

This entitlement meant that centers would take uninsured patients requiring dialysis for three months with no funding, with the understanding that after three months Medicare would kick in and the clinic would have a long-term patient. Grady, with its goal of serving the underserved, took patients with no funding and patients that no other center would take because of mental health difficulties, substance abuse, or behavior and physical issues. Since other centers in Atlanta knew Grady accepted everyone, they refused to take any uninsured patient. Thus, Grady would get all the uninsured patients in the area. The clinic had no problem in taking the patients new to dialysis and stabilizing them medically. Also, its social worker could get them funded and in three months transfer the patient to an area clinic.

In addition, since Georgia had Emergency Medicaid, those undocumented citizens and other low income, noninsured people that could not qualify for Medicare could also be treated at Grady, stabilized, insured, and sent to other centers. Grady would also provide dialysis for inmates in the Atlanta, DeKalb, and Fulton Prison Systems. This arrangement worked very well for many years, although Grady had only fourteen machines and three portable machines to treat inpatient dialysis patients. As long as Grady had between forty and fifty patients, each being dialyzed three times a week, the clinic worked well. Not only did it function well, the head nurse who had run the clinic since the beginning offered classes to train area nurses on how to become a dialysis nurse. These nurses gladly paid $2,000 for these specialized classes.

But when Georgia's Governor eliminated Emergency Medicaid in Georgia, problems became apparent. Clinics that were no longer receiving funding for those patients would discharge them and these patients would end up in Grady's Emergency Room and then in the Dialysis Clinic. Within less than a year, Grady's Dialysis Clinic had 123 full-time patients. The social worker had transferred all the patients who were funded or transferable. Grady put a freeze on all new patients and told the prison system they would have to find an alternative to provide dialysis for their prisoners. Of the 123 patients, only ten patients had any funding. These included a man who was paralyzed from the neck down and had to receive his dialysis on a stretcher, a schizophrenic, and several drug addicts, as well as those with behavior problems. In short, these included patients that other centers would not take. Nurses were working overtime and the old machines were breaking down.

The decision was made to close the dialysis clinic as it was no longer viable to stay open; it was hemorrhaging money and the machines were dying. All this was occurring at a time when Grady was in danger of closing because of its overwhelming deficit. The clinic could no longer accept any patients. Obviously, the Hospital Administration decided to close the clinic and therefore made funds available to social service to facilitate these transfers and discharges.

The social worker now had to find alternative dialysis for 123 poor, unfunded people who required this life-sustaining treatment. Due to this enormous project and the number of Spanish speaking patients, one of Grady's Hispanic social workers, Migdalia Acevedo was assigned to work in concert with the dialysis social worker. She already had contacts with the Mexican consulate and since she was a social worker in the International Clinic, she saw several of the patients in that venue. She immediately went to work with the Mexican and South American patients. In considering resources available, we found that it was easier to get a kidney transplant in Mexico than in the US. However, they only provided dialysis two times a week. She evaluated and determined which patients should be transferred back to their hometowns in Mexico and Central America.

While she worked with those patients, I looked for placements for the others. We had two patients from Jamaica, one of whom was in Grady's nursing home. And the other patient, who had been living in the United States for more than twenty years, and was working with a social security card he bought in New York when he first arrived. When I spoke to the health counsel in Jamaica, I discovered that their residents who were unable to pay for their dialysis did not receive dialysis and they certainly would not pay for the nursing home of our Jamaican lady.

Our Hispanic social worker and I would brainstorm about what to do. We researched those states that provided funding for their residents who were in this country illegally but required dialysis. We then checked with patients who had relatives in those states or had a desire to move to those states and made arrangements to get them there. We would give them money for gasoline or bus tickets to move to their relatives in those states. We would be creative in providing funds for whatever was required to move them to a place where they could receive dialysis.

Of course, not all the patients we had were undocumented citizens. In Georgia, one must wait five years after receiving one's green card before one can receive any entitlement. It takes a long time for a person to get a green card so we had legal residents who had been in this country for several years with no funding but did have green cards. One man who was born and lived in Georgia his whole life worked for the school system as a janitor. He was entitled to the same benefits as the teachers who do not pay into social security but have their own fund. When this man retired, he did not understand this and signed away his benefits. He had never paid into the Medicare fund so he did not qualify for Medicare and made too much for Medicaid. He certainly did not make enough to pay for the enormous price of dialysis. Grady had been his only option. At one point, we found a company called Mex Care that would provide a plane ticket to the individuals as well as pay for three months of dialysis in their home county. This service became very helpful.

When Grady began the process of closing their clinic, it meant unfunded people had nowhere to go to get their dialysis. They would come into Grady's Emergency Room, receive dialysis but they would not be admitted to the clinic as the clinic was closed to new patients. They could not get scheduled dialysis and their health would be at risk. Many ended up as inpatients as their health declined. Meanwhile, as Migdalia and I were trying to find solutions to this almost impossible task, people began demonstrating — saying that Grady was unfair to poor people. Community leaders would arrange demonstrations arguing that Grady was more concerned about money than about serving the poor. (For the first time in my life, I crossed a picket line to go to work.)

This resulted in a nationwide debate on whether medical care was a right or a privilege and about safety-net hospitals. Many articles appeared in local newspapers as well as in The Wall Street Journal and the New York Times. Some of the articles would interview and highlight individuals who required dialysis and were "being thrown out of Grady's dialysis." I remember an article about a young woman who had come to the Emergency Room after Grady had stopped taking patients in its clinic and the article read as if she had been in the clinic and was being thrown out. One of the protestors, who attended my synagogue, confronted me there, and asked why I was doing this to the dialysis patients.

We were able to get the census down to fifty-one people that we just could not place, including the Jamaican woman who was in Grady's nursing home because her family refused to take her. There had been a number of lawsuits filed arguing that Grady was dumping chronically ill patients that required dialysis. Because of Grady's financial situation, the court sided with Grady; they could close their center. Still, Grady had to find a solution for the fifty-one remaining patients. Since none of the other centers at that time were willing to take these people and Grady still had patients that required dialysis, they ended up with a contract with Fresenius in September 2009. Originally, this was for a year but each time the agreement would expire Grady would agree to pay Fresenius. By September 2011, the number of patients was down to twenty-one.

This final solution meant there would be no place for those difficult patients requiring dialysis to go. My thoughts were, had other centers taken some of the uninsured patients and left Grady to take those difficult or uninsured patients and keep its census down to forty or fifty people, Atlanta's dialysis community would have been better off. Perhaps I am a bit naïve. This closure occurred at a time when Grady was undergoing great change. Grady's dialysis center would never be able to break even financially, so it remained a drain on Grady's budget during my tenure there.

MY LIFE AS A SOCIAL WORK ADMINISTRATOR

Charlene Turner

Being a social work administrator in a large urban, teaching hospital has many rewards along with its challenges. Overall, the rewards far outweigh the challenges. Many people questioned how I stayed in the position for 40 years – my answer was that I had the best social work job in the city. It was truly a labor of love.

I was initially hired as a staff social worker, quickly became a supervisor, and within a year; I found myself in the director's role. In my previous job in a mental health center, my supervisory experience was limited to supervising a social work student and a community worker. So, this novice manager was now in charge of a department that had supposedly "forced" the previous director to quit abruptly and had been without a permanent director for over a year. I was told by a senior executive that the department consisted of a "bunch of whining brats" who did not want to work. While I did not find this to be completely true, I did find a splintered department with individuals who felt unappreciated and overworked-and somewhat resistant to working with this newly arrived MSW. At that time, the department consisted primarily of bachelor level workers of various backgrounds. It took considerable time and effort to establish a level of trust with the staff and I came close to resigning several times when I felt overwhelmed with continued staff grievances.

Much of the discontent was related to salary and the heavy workload. Workers covered two or three different inpatient areas and all the clinics. In addition, workers had to cover the ER on a rotating basis and also work on Saturdays and holidays. At this time (1972-73), the department had less than ten social workers, including the director. I also worked an area, sometimes not leaving the hospital until late evening. So, I put on my "advocacy" hat with the intent of getting more staff and an increase in their salary. First, I went to my administrator who punted me to the head of Personnel (now called Human Resources). The reception from that department was unforgettable as the sentiment voiced was to "tell those workers they can leave and let the door hit them where the sun does not shine." Naturally, I could not let the staff know the sentiment: so I had to work through their feeling that I had not advocated effectively. Parenthetically, I should mention that this department head would only talk with me when a meeting had been pre-arranged by my administrator. I concluded that my "blackness" was the reason I had difficulty in arranging meetings. However, a subsequent conversation with a black member of that department convinced me that I had reached the wrong conclusion. Perhaps my reception was related more to the fact that I was so new to the system.

Despite the staffing issues and general discontent, I had strong administrative support from the beginning which bolstered my confidence. The CEO (the late J. W. Pinkston) actually interviewed me for the job and remained supportive throughout his tenure. This support even extended to the Board of Trustees at the time. I will never forget my fear and trepidation the first time I had to present the department's budget before the board. I had been warned about the Board Chairman, the late Dr. Edward C. Loughlin, Jr., and how he could be very intimidating. He asked me two questions—and I answered each one in a shaky, trembling voice. Whatever I said must have been sufficient as he later advised me that he had deposited a large sum of money into our Social Service Emergency Fund. Before he left the Board, he gave me his personal phone number and asked that I call him if I ever needed any favors. He gave our department a compliment which I never forgot—"Social Service is the conscience of the hospital." This same kind of administrative support continued through most of my tenure—particularly true of two other CEOs (Mr. Ed Renford and Mr. Mike Young). I might mention that I worked under ten different CEOs during my tenure-each with their own perspective about social work. Two of those CEOs had social work backgrounds (Wilson and Stephenson), otherwise, I found myself having to educate the leaders about our work and how we helped patients.

A number of resignations came in those early years, which led to the hiring of new staff who came with renewed energy. Subsequently, I was able to hire more master's prepared workers. It could be said that the department went through a "rebuilding" stage before we moved forward in a more cohesive, productive fashion-but this took several years. Our best marketing tool was the demonstration of quality service provision to our patients and families. We became known as the department to go to when "something" needed to be done to benefit our patients.

One of the most trying experiences during this time (late 80s) was a major change in leadership and the advent of a department known as Management Engineering. This department was known as the "fix-it" group and fixing it generally resulted in the termination of the department head. Our time of review arrived and we nervously began a period of intense scrutiny. The results of our review were astounding —we got high marks in all areas! Their written report validated our department in all areas and they even recommended that we be given more staff in certain areas. However, the internal review eventually gave way to the external consultants as the hospital had major financial difficulties. Naturally, social work was always subject to extra scrutiny as we were seen as non-revenue producing. Again, the department survived, but not without the help of some major allies in the system. While we had support from nursing, finance, and other departments— our greatest ally was the medical staff. The department continued to grow and thrive. At one point, the department had over one hundred workers. We were able to have workers specialize in certain areas and we had 24-hour coverage in the ER. We even established our own "pool" of workers to cover when the regular staff was absent for a period of time and these pool workers were used to cover weekends and holidays. We added social work assistants to the department and they were useful in relieving the MSWs from certain tasks, especially in the ER. Given this abundance of staff, social workers were able to provide much-needed counseling and support to patients and families

—and still focus on discharge planning. The various departments even began to "demand" and make known how they needed their own social worker. Our department was well respected throughout the system.

During the middle phase of my tenure, we seemingly coasted along, providing service to patients as needed in the hospital community. We had a dedicated core of supervisors for each major service area, a strong assistant director, and strong support throughout the hospital. We had developed major connections with the various community resources and could generally get the needs of our patients met. We had strong ties to the local schools of social work and were a major placement resource for Georgia State, Clark Atlanta, the University of Georgia, and later Kennesaw State. The schools viewed Grady as a valuable training ground for their students and sent them to us in large numbers. Many of the students were later hired in the department. If they were not hired in our department, many were hired in other local hospitals; so we had lots of connections in other hospitals throughout the state.

In the late 90s, our department was merged with Utilization Review and Nurse Case Managers (as a result of a recommendation from one of the outside consultants). This merger and the endless territorial issues added considerable stress to my life and the department as a whole. For starters, the Utilization Review staff (most were nurses) did not have the same training as the nurse case managers and were more accustomed to reading charts and talking to payers; while the nurse case managers were more adept at bedside nursing and talking to patients and not familiar with getting payments from insurance companies. To make matters worse, the nurse case managers were at a higher pay grade than the UR nurses and social workers. Most of the Utilization Review staff left or transferred to other areas, and that left the nurse case managers in a position where they had to learn the UR function in a "hurry". New supervisors were hired for the nurses and we proceeded to merge them with the social work supervisors. We had to work through considerable conflict and there were many tense moments. At one point, the conflict reached such a high level that the entire supervisory staff was sent to the hospital mediator for conflict resolution. All the while, I had to walk a fine line. Otherwise, I would be accused of favoring the social work staff over the nurses. This happened on more than one occasion.

It took a couple of years for the department to gel and begin working together as mature professionals. Eventually, social workers were paired with nurse case managers for the inpatient areas —and ongoing problems were dealt with as they arose. The underlying sentiment of the social workers was that they knew more about resources and could deal with complex issues much better than the nurses; while the nurses generally felt their clinical expertise allowed them to do discharge planning more expeditiously. Given these somewhat different perspectives, one can imagine that it would take some time for these two groups to begin to respect each other for their unique value (and the salary difference was a factor that did not help).

There were two other rocky periods in my tenure of note—both of those times related to mandates to reduce the length of stay. On both occasions, supervisors were hired into the system and put over Social Service and each time I attempted to adjust to the new reporting structure. However, in both cases, the social work approach to discharge planning and working with patients, in general, was not valued —so I found myself in almost daily battles. At one point, I was removed from work on the inpatient side and was instructed to focus solely on the outpatient clinics. Again, I came close to resigning but stayed after my daughter flippantly stated that she never knew her mother was a quitter.

On another occasion, I was moved out of the department and relocated to a remote area of the hospital. I had always maintained an open-door policy and this made me generally inaccessible to staff. These experiences left me with some battle-scars, but ultimately they strengthened my resolve to stay focused and true to my profession.

Back in the year 2000, the department was renamed the Care Management Department and I was promoted to the position of Administrative Director, with a Director of Social Service and a Director of Case Management reporting to me. I reported to Dr. Curtis Lewis and Howard Mosby in the Division of Medical Affairs where our department had strong support for a number of years.

A couple of years before I retired, our department was switched to the Finance Division and I found myself in a "foreign land." After a short span of time in this division, my position was eliminated and I ultimately retired. My retirement was long overdue, as I had announced my intent to retire years earlier. However, when I assembled the social workers and made the announcement – we all had a crying party to the extent that a staff member (not one of the social workers) called one of my daughters and told her that the social workers were acting like I had passed away. I can now truly say with many others –"there is life after Grady." I have no regrets about my time at Grady and can look back on my career there with pride and a sense of accomplishment.

GAME CHANGER MOMENTS AND EVENTS

Charlene Turner

A Call to Lunch

After about six months on the job as director, I was invited to lunch by the head of the MEC (the Medical Emergency Center). The person in charge was an African American nurse, Ramona Andrews, who was well respected throughout the hospital. So, this rookie director was excited to have lunch with this important person. We did the usual chitchat and then she assumed a very serious tone. She proceeded to tell me that I should stop wearing the black, brown, and navy clothes that I normally wore, put on some makeup and earrings, and get some different stockings. I listened very carefully and respectfully told her I could do one or two of the things she suggested- but not everything. She was somewhat disappointed in my response and proceeded to tell me the history of black nurses at the hospital. She delivered the message that it was vitally important for me to present myself in a certain way. I tried to change my style -but it was hard to overcome those childhood messages that black folk should not wear bright colors. It took me about twenty years to get past some of those old messages—and the folk who observed me in the latter part of my career probably tired of seeing me in my red, purple, or gold suits. During our years of working together, Ms. Andrews would only be partially satisfied, as I still could not do the earrings or makeup.

The Valuables Incident

I was sitting in a meeting with a new Grady CEO who was telling the group what he knew about the hospital prior to his arrival. One of the statements he made was this: "And I understand that you have social workers who steal jewelry off of dead people." All of the eyes in the room turned towards me —and I just dropped my head. Social Service had the responsibility of collecting valuables as patients came into the ER. We were then to transport the valuables to the Security Department.

There was a definite protocol outlined for this process—but not as airtight as we thought. One of our staff was accused of taking valuable jewelry from the body of a deceased patient. The patient's spouse gave a vivid description of the item—and demanded its return. When it was not immediately found-he went to the news media and it was front-page news for several days. Somehow, the jewelry ended up in a pawnshop. Security and law enforcement handled the case from that point. Needless to say, from that point on the Security Department handled all valuables —which is where the responsibility should have been in the first place. This was a dark moment in the history of our department.

Development of a "Diligent Search" Protocol
Perhaps unique to a hospital such as Grady, social workers had the responsibility of locating/notifying the next of kin for admitted patients —whether the patient was dead or alive. After a few missteps with these situations, we designed what we considered a mistake-proof tool for use in these circumstances. With one of these "missteps", our department (and the hospital) was featured in the local newspaper as not having made a diligent search to notify a relative of a deceased patient. I actually went out to visit the family to make an apology and try to explain what happened—and had to absorb all of the negative comments from the family. After this incident, I was committed never again to be in this situation, where we have to explain how or why we had not made timely notification.

So, we developed a format that required all boxes on a form to be checked to indicate a thorough search had been done. We would even contact police officials for fingerprints whenever we had a John Doe or a Jane Doe. We would make visits to the community as needed in the effort to identify patients. Assistant Director, Doll Adams, and I once visited a park where a John Doe had been found. We observed several workers in the area and gave them a description of our patient - no one seemed to know our patient and most of them spoke little English. We left a card and later received a call that the patient was one of the "boat people" who had come over from Cuba. The caller provided enough information for us to locate the patient's adopted family who had been trying to find him.

Decedent Affairs Office
Again, due to more than one misstep in the release of bodies, a multidisciplinary problem-solving group established the Decedent Affairs Office (which became another addition to our social service responsibilities). We were to ensure that all the proper steps were taken in the release of bodies - to make sure the right body was released and properly signed out to the funeral home. This position required almost daily interaction with the Pathology Department and the local medical examiner's office to ensure proper authorization for autopsies, location of next of kin, and completion of proper paperwork to ensure timely disposal of remains. It was not unusual to have to deal with family conflict over who was going to sign a body out of the hospital.

I distinctly remember a case of a patient who had three wives. One of our administrators was also an ordained minister and he had performed one of the marriages. Can you imagine his surprise when he was informed that the wife he validated was not the legal wife? Our first Decedent Affairs Officer, Emerson Ross, had a military background and brought that knowledge to bear in the development of policies for this area. My very first administrator loved to tell the story of how we sent a "black" body to a white funeral home and created quite an uproar. I can say we had no major mishaps once this office was up and running —but it did require attention to detail and some strong advocacy at times. Mr. Ross' unique style was perfect for this assignment.

Initiation of "the Long Stay Board"
Under the leadership of the Medical Director and the Vice President of Medical Affairs, Dr. Curtis Lewis and Howard Mosby, we were instrumental in establishing this committee to identify and focus on patients with discharge issues that would lead to extended stays in the hospital and adversely affect the hospital's bottom line. Dr. Lewis and

Mr. Mosby co-chaired the group and social work presented the patients who had long stays in the hospital. We led the brainstorming effort in how to overcome the barriers to discharge. Overall, this group was very successful and able to make a significant reduction in the hospital's length of stay and the board continues to this day with the same focus. The various hospital leaders who were on this board gained a better appreciation of the challenges involved in facilitating difficult discharges in a timely manner and a better understanding of social work.

A Call to Action

There was a call to action when I learned (covertly) that a consultant group had recommended that the social work department be cut by two-thirds. My informant provided enough information to let me know that the CEO at that time was planning to follow the recommendation. Doll Adams, my Assistant Director, and I strategized one evening and came up with a plan of action. A "secret" meeting was held with our most trusted staff members who were told of the recommendation and how we needed to respond. The plan was to get a petition to all of our leading physicians and ask them to sign their names indicating their support for social work and their concern about any possible cuts in our staff. Somehow, the petition landed on the desk of the CEO —and the medical staff went even further and demanded an emergency meeting with the CEO. I was not in attendance but got a report that the docs gave "testimonials" about the value of our department. The CEO later said to me that he never intended to cut our staff.

The Tornado

The administrator on duty called me one Saturday night and informed me that my office was damaged by a tornado that came through downtown Atlanta. I was baffled as to how my office could have possibly been damaged as it was an inner office with no windows. However, when I arrived at work on Monday, I found my office cordoned off with a black tarp and when I peeped inside, I saw the damage. It turned out that a huge concrete block had fallen from the 16th floor through the floor of my office on the first floor all the way to the basement. Everything in my office had gotten wet —including my shoes. For some strange reason, I kept a huge cardboard box under my desk that contained about thirty pairs of shoes and I was never able to get all of them back in good shape. I had to move temporarily down the hall to Administration –but I took the shoes that were still wearable with me.

Other Duties as Assigned
Before the hospital established a Patient Advocate Office, Social Service normally handled the various patient complaints. Since we were located down the hall from Administration, I routinely received referrals of upset patients or families -this led to my working directly with most administrators over the years. In many ways, I became "the social worker" for the hospital, as other department directors would also refer their employees who were experiencing problems of all kinds. I remember distinctly working with an elderly gentleman who had worked in Food Service for many years and somehow was in dire financial straits. Due to his last name, I guessed that he was related to a well-known basketball star –and yes, he was the uncle of that player. However, he was a proud man and would not allow me to contact his nephew on his behalf. On occasion, employees would come to me on their own. One such employee was a lady who worked in the Finance area and was known for the way she questioned department heads about their budgets. I helped her with a simple matter –and from that point on –she gave me a "lot of needed grace" in all budgetary matters. Once we had a patient fatally shot in the hospital by a police officer, Mr. Ed Renford, the CEO immediately asked me to work with the family of the deceased patient. I could go on and on about these other duties as assigned- daily unpredictable occurrences that required on-the-spot assessments and decisive action on behalf of the hospital.

Establishment of the Pharmacy Advisory Board
In the late 90s, a decision was made to increase the price of medication. As the community learned of the increase, community groups began protests outside the hospital –and on occasion, would march into the administrative suite. Whenever they entered that area, I was normally called to join administrators and meet with the protesters. On one such

occasion, I stood between the CEO and the COO. The lead protester came up and grabbed my hand and loudly proclaimed, "We have at least one honest person in the room". They were not aware of the fact that I had worked with this person at his church providing outreach services to HIV patients. The tension between the community and the hospital was extremely high, so I decided that something had to be done to get both sides really talking and negotiating. So, I went to the CEO and got his blessings to start a "pharmacy advisory board." The board consisted of representation from the pharmacy and other key hospital staff, as well as several of the community activist who had been most outspoken against the pharmacy. One of the most outspoken critics, in the beginning, became one of the pharmacy's biggest advocates over time. The board met regularly and discussed all the issues involved with the proposed price increases –and ultimately came to a compromised solution as to how the price increases should proceed.

The Funeral
Mr. W was Doll Adams' regular patients. He was known throughout the hospital as he came often and rode on the hospital's non-emergency van. He died and the whole department was saddened by his loss. We wanted to remember him in a special way. There was no immediate family, so we decided that a special funeral service was in order. Our longtime receptionist, Ruby Porter had a special relationship with Stocks Funeral Home and arranged complimentary services for the patient - including the use of a chapel for the service. Ms. Adams played the piano and James Reed sang a solo. Remarks were given by hospital staff who knew Mr. W well - and when the van driver made his remarks about their trips together – our longtime receptionist and I began to weep as if we were the closest of family. Mr. W would have been pleased. We "put him away in style".

The Homeless Challenge
There was a time when Grady's ER was almost overwhelmed with homeless persons who knew this was a place where they could get some rest from the street. In order to remain in the ER for a while, many

of them would present with "toe aches, back pain, or whatever and the medical staff would be obligated to check their condition. Two different CEOs decided I needed to correct this problem of overutilization of the ER and were not shy about letting the rest of the hospital know that this was a "social service" problem. One of them would openly call me out in Department Heads' Meeting and openly ask what I was doing to solve the homeless problem. On one occasion, I stopped him before he went into the meeting and asked that he not call me out in the meeting —and he nodded in agreement.

Five minutes into the meeting, he announced to the group that I had asked him not to call on me in the meeting —but he was going to do it anyway. The CEO who followed next picked up the same banner and was even more adamant about the charge he gave me to solve the problem. I decided to take a different approach with this CEO and get the assistance of some of the homeless advocates in the community. I started a monthly "breakfast with the CEO" where we all joined forces in educating the CEO about all the issues surrounding the homeless problem in Atlanta and brainstorming about how to resolve some of the issues. Naturally, Social Service did not totally resolve the homeless issue-but we helped. We facilitated a better connection between the various community resources to the extent that there was less reliance on the ER for shelter. Much credit goes to Mercy Care, Odyssey 111, Crossroads, United Way, and others who answered my call for help. Some of the partnerships started in this effort have remained to this day. I was actually given an award from Mercy Care for my efforts in working with the homeless issue at Grady.

The Last Ride
Our night social worker, Jim Hammons made me aware of a most unusual case situation in the ER. The husband of a deceased patient requested to transport his deceased wife to a funeral home in Florida. He was a truck driver who was making a cross-country trip when his wife became ill, he stopped in Atlanta and was directed to our ER. He was driving an eighteen-wheeler refrigerated truck and insisted that he would go directly to a funeral home in Florida. Plus, he stated that this

would have been his wife's desire. There was much discussion about the rules and regulations about the transport of a body across the state line —and consultation with the Health Department, the Medical Examiner's Office and several other agencies —and Grady finally had to make a decision. One of our longtime nurse night administrators who weighed less than 100 pounds helped rearrange the items inside the truck and then helped with loading the deceased body in the truck. We checked later in the day; and sure enough, the body had arrived at the designated funeral home.

Retirement Parties
When word got out about my upcoming retirement, staff members began preparing a retirement party. But, when Jeannette Swann-Dean in Administration learned about the plans—she took charge. What a party —the Grady Auditorium was packed to standing room only. There were folk there who were at Grady when I first started in 1972. The highlight of the party was the brief comments from most of the CEOs I had worked with through the years —the ones who were not in attendance spoke by video. I was especially honored to have Mr. Ed Renford, former CEO, (we had a great working relationship) come and offer comments in his usual memorable and unique style. He told me that this was his first time back at Grady since he left. I have no idea how Jeannette was able to contact all of the folk that were there —and yes, the Chairman of the Board was also present. It was truly a party for the ages!

There was another party off campus a few days later and this one was coordinated by two special social workers (Maranda Randolph and Felicia English). It was a formal affair with many of the attendees coming from out of town. One social worker came from Florida and stood up to tell folk how I had not hired her as a supervisor and came to regret that decision —I was amazed that she, Ann Simpson, had been waiting all these years to tell that story. It was at this party that I announced plans to write a book — and Dr. Neil Shulman, a famous Grady doc and writer offered to help with any book writing effort. I will never forget either party.

GENTRIFICATION ATLANTA STYLE

Louise Spiro

Mrs. W was a widow who attended Grady's Geriatric Clinic. Her husband had been very domineering prior to his death and Mrs. W was trying to adjust to living alone. One would think she was a homeless woman by the way she presented herself. She was a very small woman with wild white hair who wore old, mismatched clothes and walked slowly with a limp. However, Mrs. W was a homeowner who received her husband's pension. She lived across the street from Milton Avenue homeless shelter. This shelter had an infirmary staffed by a Nurse Practitioner who had contacted me about Mrs. W. Every day she would go across the street at lunchtime for a meal. Normally these were meals only for the homeless but they made an exception for this lady as she looked and acted so pathetic. However, the nurse was concerned about her because of her lifestyle.

When I attempted to make a home visit to see what was happening, I was denied entrance to Mrs. W home. I could not see inside her home as the windows were blocked with things. She had 3 cars in her front yard all filled to the top with stuff. If a person wanted to get into these cars, they couldn't, due to the amount of stuff in them. To say Mrs. W was a hoarder, was an understatement. This behavior began following the death of her husband. I went across the street to talk to the nurse in the shelter. She informed me that 6 months before my visit, the neighborhood had gotten together to clean out Mrs. W's house and property to have it within a few weeks to totally returned to the prior state. This nurse further informed me about her real concern. The neighborhood was in the process of gentrification and there had been a number of suspicious fires in this neighborhood with the end result of properties being sold cheaply. Due to Mrs. W's vulnerability, the nurse feared Mrs. W's house may be next.

When I returned to my office, I attempted to call various contacts I had to see if I could help Mrs. W to no avail. Legal Aid and housing didn't believe this was a real threat. I had attempted to locate other family members to no avail. She did not have any children and denied other relatives. After months of trying to find contacts to help this lady, she tells me she is planning on taking a trip for Christmas. I asked her where she was going and she replies, "to Waycross, Georgia to visit relatives. Relatives that she had denied having in the past. While she was away, her house caught fire and was burned to the ground. With her house gone, Mrs. W revealed she had $50,000 hidden under her mattress which went up in the fire. I'm not sure what the outcome of her loss was, but her relatives moved her to Waycross closer to them.

On the west side of town, near Atlanta University complex, I had another patient who was 82 years old and had been renting the same house for over 40 years. When I had visited her, the house was in terrible disrepair. I was fearful her ceiling was going to collapse on her. I tried to get help for her in repairing her home. When she came crying to me that she was being evicted from her home, I was certain that the health department had condemned the building. I was wrong. The owners had sold the house to developers. I began looking for alternative housing for this lady, but before I could get too far, she had a massive stroke and died. I do not doubt that having to leave her home after 40 years lead to this stroke.

REFLECTIONS: THE METAMORPHOSIS OF A NEOPHYTE

Vickie Ogunlade

INTRODUCTION

Gingerly I entered the door- not sure of why I was so hesitant since this was not the first time that I had visited Grady's Office of Social Services. I glanced around. Sitting at the receptionist's desk was a woman, an elder who greeted me with a warm smile, quickly responding to a demanding phone, while simultaneously paying respectful attention to the line of geriatric patients seated along the wall. Later I understood that they were arriving from the Medical Walk-in Clinic to see the clinic social worker- me.

No, Grady Memorial Hospital was not new to me. This familiarity was not because I was born at "the Gradys", for I was delivered at one of the only two private hospitals for African Americans during 1955 – Hugh Spaulding. Instead Grady was a part of my earlier life through the experiences of my mother, Dorothy Phyllis Canady Benjamin. A registered nurse, Mrs. Benjamin was a graduate of the Grady Colored School for Nurses (1950) (Georgia State University Library, (2020) and Auburn Avenue Research Library (2020). She returned to Grady, a county hospital to serve the community, after working in various health facilities from Ashville North Carolina to Atlanta, Georgia. Her belief in public service was embedded in our family. I remembered the Grady emergency room on early Sunday mornings, as my mom, took her break to greet my daddy and I, as she quickly braided my hair and tied ribbons so I would look "just right" for church service. After walking from a nearby Catholic school, I experienced the Grady pediatric outpatient clinic waiting room; chatting with other children, while completing my homework, as my mother worked alongside pediatricians, well past 4:30pm. I knew Grady as a teen volunteer. I walked the 9th floor without hesitation to help sick children, finally learning to assist nursing aids with the changing of bed sheets for children with burns. As a pre-college summer intern with the Grady Family Planning Summer Program, I was able to embrace a deeper understanding of bio-psychosocial economic disparities and life challenges faced by African American women and family systems. During the following summer, as I grappled with a decision to return to Duke University for my 2nd year, I further saw Grady and the life experiences of patients through my encounters as a front-line information clerk. Providing rotating shift coverage, I helped those who entered the hospital's main entrance. During the evening and overnight shifts I found myself in a glass booth between the MEC (Medical Emergency Clinic) and the SEC (Surgical Emergency Clinic). I watched emergencies roll in, was witness to the pain of significant others, and heard their sobs; while I took death calls and notified funeral homes to receive into their care those who had transcended. Several summers later I returned to Grady Hospital. Without hesitation, I provided weekly onsite supervisory sessions of Job Corp summer interns developing skills, while embedded in the department of medical records. Later, with my newly acquired skills as a first-year MSW social work student, I interviewed elders in the community, which required knowledge of this public hospital, known to so many as the Gradys.

So, here I was – entering the Office of Social Services. I had successfully completed a block internship within a major health facility, and received my MSW, with a specialization in Hospital Social Work. With a history of varied encounters over the years within the world of Grady, and confident as a long-term member of the Metro Atlanta community, I just knew that I was ready for my first position as a master's level medical social worker. Indeed - so one would think there was no reason for hesitancy, as I crossed the threshold of the department. However, there was: Though a MSW graduate, I was a neophyte. A novice in the field walking forward to face daily expectations, to embrace human needs and determine processes, which were to be of value to patients in dire need of ethical, critical, and effective social services. I was shaken, as I learned of my responsibility to work with the elders who were patiently waiting for their clinic social worker to arrive. This was quite evident to my seasoned supervisor, who quickly sat at my desk, to encourage me to "hang in there". As a part of this process, she shared a short poem, with the picture of a turtle struggling to keep its head above water. I was left wondering how soon I would drown. However, I endured, evolving over time. As a compassionate, committed, and ethical clinician, with an expanding skill-set, I came to realize my capabilities, humbly recognizing that I was indeed of value to those who needed effective medical social work services.

THE EMERGENCE

My tenure with Grady Hospital was a ten-year experience (1979-1989). I was able to move beyond the social worker who primarily provided information and referrals, to one who daily carved out time to therapeutically listen and provide emotional support in the midst of admissions, and during busy clinic appointments. Overtime my confidence increased. Present in medical team rounds or the recipient of face-to-face referrals, I never referenced my patients as their diagnoses. Instead, I acknowledged their human presence, as well as their position as honored elders. Also, as a social worker assigned to teams, with an operational foundation of cultural sensitivity and respect, I embraced the need and challenge to educate interdisciplinary team members regarding patients' psycho-social economic dynamics, which impacted their medical issues. This was not an easy task to execute, for oftentimes, I was seen as "just the social worker." However, nestled in a department where clinicians honored their role and functioned as advocates, without hesitation I saw each case through these lenses. Subsequently, educational encounters manifested in various settings, ranging from formal team meetings to cornerstone consultations. Each day I walked through the doors of Grady Memorial Hospital, with a deepening understanding of how my roles and functions (NASW, 2016) impacted patients' lives and their medical care. I accepted demanding responsibilities and executed significant tasks, which were critical in support of patients, as well as significant others who assumed the role and functions of caregiving. Services were rendered to patients either hospitalized, in the process of planning for discharge, anticipating life's transition without hospice care, or living within the community with acute or chronic illnesses.

My professional metamorphosis as a medical social worker occurred overtime, driven by challenging experiences. This process was undergirded by varied supervisory relationships, collegial affiliations, as well as multidisciplinary encounters. I emerged from my initial day of employment with the realization that my supervisory relationship was a core element of my new professional life. Within the first months of service delivery I knew without a doubt that in my role as a medical social worker, I was professionally in need of and reliant upon my supervisors' time, knowledge, and guidance for:

- A preliminary and practical understanding of this physical institution, the inter-twining systems, and multidisciplinary relationships.
- The development of a functional knowledge base and skill-set based upon departmental policies and procedures vital for the provision of effective social work services.
- My professional survival as a neophyte medical social worker in the largest health care facility for the high risk, in North Georgia. With each new supervisory relationship, I experienced profound opportunities of professional growth. This metamorphic process also encompassed professional challenges, with trials and errors: This led to a questioning of my decision to become a social worker. However, with the eruption of humility I endured; supported and encouraged by colleagues who also walked the Grady concrete floors.

As a 'newbie' I was impacted by the rule of seniority within my 1st five months. On Christmas Day, I sat in the office, as the sole social worker to cover medical and surgical emergency clinics (MEC/SEC).

Back then coverage for the inpatient areas was not a requirement. The phones were quiet, and the office was empty. Then a call came through - I was needed in the MEC.

There she was, standing in a seat, expressing herself loudly, arms freely swinging, while shaking her torso back and forth. She was there to see a doctor. I was there to "talk" her down. I had watched her come through the Social Services office on the first floor. A tall full-figured woman, she was usually in true form, wearing her personalized outfits, with hairstyles and make-up most would describe as bizarre. Her arrival in the main Social Service office was sporadic, for she was "followed" by psychiatry (commonly known as "the 8th Floor" in 1979). Some days she demanded control of the waiting area, expressing herself in a manner that required a confident response. At times, I was lucky enough to observe seasoned clinicians, as they responded to her presence with a respect for her needs. Despite her ability to disrupt the total environment, occasionally she would sit quietly, feet together, hands folded, while surveying the room, as she waited for assistance. Also, on one of those quiet days, as I walked by en route to my office, she noticed me and spoke.

So, she was the person in the MEC, on this Christmas Day. She presented "in charge" in true form, as she made known her presence. As I softly greeted her by name, Ms. S. paused in that moment, while surveying the scene and taking note of this 24-year-old social worker. I was unsure if she remembered me from the office, but Ms. S. calmed down as we engaged in a conversation of her creation. This was the day I truly experienced how to be present with a patient (regardless of the state of mind), starting where she was and allowing her to process our collective plan of action. As I returned to the office, drained, with a strong desire to be home with my family, I was left wondering if Ms. S' people were missing her at their table on this special day. Years later I saw Ms. S. in the community, on Auburn Avenue. She waved and hollered "hey".

AREAS OF PRACTICE
Practicing within the Grady environment was a powerful experience. Working across various areas proved to be the catalyst for a level of professional growth beyond personal expectations. Areas of practice encompassed:
- Ambulatory Medical Clinics; Obstetrics, Gynecology, Gynecology-Tumor (1979-1982)
- Geriatrics and Emergency Services (1982-1983)
- The Georgia Sickle Cell Center (1982-1987)
- General Pediatrics (1987-1988)
- Rehabilitation Medicine (1989)
- Practicum Supervision (1980-1989)

Furthermore, supervisory relationships, clinical peer consultation, intra/inter-departmental meetings, multidisciplinary discussions, and silent observations stimulated, supported, and oftentimes drove my progression in skill enhancement. Progression was reflected in the following areas:
- An increase in personal and professional patience.
- An understanding of politics, inter/intra departmental politics as well as between community agencies, which impacted the lives of patients and the delivery of critical social services.
- The need for and the value of data and outcomes for program planning.
- The development and respect for informal and formal multidisciplinary relationships.
- An awareness of the psychosocial sequalae of chronic or acute medical conditions endured by patients in assigned practice areas.
- Professional skills to develop psychosocial educational tools for patients.
- The ability to share my professional skills via the MSW practicum experience.

The following is an example of a significant supervisory relationship which shifted my course as a medical social worker:

Based on my previous work in the Grady Family Planning Program, as well as my OB/GYN block practicum within a university hospital, during my initial year at Grady, I began an inquiry, with the hope of being a part of the OB/GYN team. My encounter with the supervisor of the OB/GYN Unit was meaningful: It resulted in the development of a teaching relationship, enhancing my appreciation of proposals, data outcomes, justifications, and interdepartmental collaborations. I was given the responsibility to glean critical statistics, which revealed how many referred patients lacked social work support services over a selected period, because of limited staffing. As of result of this study, the supervisor was able to bring me on board as a second social worker for the unit. As a team, the OB/GYN social workers established and maintained inter-departmental relationships and collaborations, which supported the following outcomes over a three-year period:

- The development of social work protocols, with the creation and implementation of groups for the OB outpatient clinic setting.
- The development and implementation of protocols for the provision of sensitive supportive social work services and coordination of crisis placements during an era of "closed" adoptions in the state of Georgia.
- The coordination of in-patient coverage to effect death and dying counseling from an individual and family system perspective, for inpatient GYN Tumor patients not enrolled in the Grady Hospice Program.

CLINICAL REFLECTION

Reflections regarding my clinical practice at Grady Hospital revealed that I found it difficult to accept "no" or "not at this time" when I perceived a need for planning and programming for the benefit of my patient population. Such was manifested during my tenure with the Sickle Cell Center, where I sought out different methods to enhance service provision. As the first full-time social worker for the Sickle Cell Clinic and the subsequent NIH Sickle Cell Center, I provided social work support for all individuals (family systems and significant others) across the life cycle – inpatient, outpatient, and during emergency visits.

During my tenure with the Center, I was also able to employ my enhanced skills-set, in collaboration with the Sickle Cell administrative multidisciplinary team and Social Service administrators, for the improvement of the availability and accessibility of social services. Data outcomes reflected gaps in service delivery and expressed needs of those impacted. The respect of this data resulted in the acquisition of a well-experienced pediatric social worker. She embraced service delivery responsibilities associated with the Sickle Cell Center clinic and the inpatient needs of the pediatric and adolescent client systems. Also, without hesitation, she joined in collaborative multidisciplinary activities beyond case management and discharge planning.

Practice in the Sickle Cell Center occurred across the spectrum: Such as discharge planning, supportive emotional counseling of client systems - inpatient and outpatient, grief counseling; psychosocial educational group services and community-based psychosocial educational workshops and professional presentations; consultations with teachers and employers regarding the potential impact of the Sickle Cell disease process, daily rounds with the Sickle Cell medical team, multidisciplinary team meetings and consultations, and periodic home visits as needed.

Program planning and implementation occurred in the following areas of practice.
- The initiation of full-time social service program design and implementation with a focus on out-patient bio-psychosocial education to enhance patients/ parents/ significant others'' knowledge and use of coping/ adaptive skills, as well as compliance with recommended treatment regimens.
- Development and implementation of stress reduction group sessions within the clinic setting and parenting groups within the community.
- Data collection and analysis to support an increase in social work staff for the Sickle Cell pediatric and adolescent populations.
- Established membership in the Sickle Cell Disease New Born Screening Task Force, composed of county, hospital, community agencies and grass-root advocates, whose efforts

supported the early provision of newborn screening to detect Sickle Cell Disease and the eventual inclusion of Sickle Cell Disease as a legislated component of the State of Georgia's newborn screening process.
- Social work community outreach, with local health fair participation and organized presentations to enhance an understanding of the psycho-social sequelae of sickle cell disease within community agencies who provided services to individuals and families impacted by Sickle Cell.
- Peer-reviewed publication pertaining to the impact of law and policy on the delivery of social services in the realm of newborn screening and sickle cell disease. (Ogunlade, 1988)

CONCLUSION

I entered the Grady Memorial Hospital Social Services Department as a neophyte, with hesitation and doubt in my ability to be of service as a medical social worker, within a public hospital. Yet, over a ten-year period, I was able to step forward. I sought out and accepted challenging assignments; experienced interactions, which altered my perceptions and subsequent ways of practicing, leading to the development and implementation of interventions beyond the micro/mezzo levels of service delivery. I emerged with skills that enhanced my value for patients who depended heavily upon my service delivery, as they wrangled with life issues complicated by medical challenges. I was also able to contribute to the profession while sharing my skill set as a practicum supervisor.

I am grateful for my personal Grady Memorial Hospital experience. For it is my belief that my Grady experience lead to an overarching metamorphosis – a process which would not have been experienced in any other setting.

ACKNOWLEDGEMENTS:

I would like to acknowledge the following individuals who had a profound impact on my professional path from neophyte to a professional medical social worker:

Amelia Williams, MSW, my OB/GYN supervisor, Marjorie Hampton, MSW and Janice Coye, LCSW, my OB/GYN colleagues – collectively they provided consultation and direction, which set me on my path as a creative medical social worker.

Yvonne Aldridge, MSW, Sickle Cell Center Social Work, a colleague whose creative consultation supported the Sickle Cell Center community-based parenting workshops.

Phyllis Canady Benjamin, RN, a Sickle Cell Genetic Counselor, who demonstrated the meaning of Service Leadership and the value of multidisciplinary consultation and program design.

Professor Hattie Mitchell, MSW, while allowing me to train her as my replacement in the Sickle Cell Center shared clinical wisdom which has sustained me over 30 years.

Charlene Turner, LCSW, the Director of the Social Service Department, who took a chance with a neophyte who did not experience a Grady Memorial Hospital MSW practicum.

REFERENCES:

Auburn Avenue Research Library on African-American Culture and History. Fulton County Library System (2020). National conclave of Grady graduate nurses collection, archives division, collection identifier: aarl05-001. https://aspacestagingaafa.galileo.usg.edu/repositories/2/resources/125

Georgia Department of Public Health Department. (2019). History of the newborn screening program in Georgia, PDF. https://dph.georgia.gov/NBS

Georgia State University Library, (2020). Digital collections: Grady municipal training school for colored nurses class, Atlanta, Georgia, 1930, Identifier: L1984-47_00. digitalcollections.library.gsu.edu

National Association of Social Workers, (2016). NASW standards for social work practice in health care settings. www.socialworkers.org

Ogunlade, V. (1988). High—risk infants and the newborn screening law: Policy implications and its impact upon social workers as case managers. Implementing Solutions to Problems of Infant Mortality and Morbidity, A Bi-Regional Conference May 13-16, 1987 Proceedings, 67-77. Chapel Hill, NC: Department of Maternal and Child Health School of Public Health / UNC@ Chapel Hill and Office of Maternal and Child Health, Bureau of Maternal and Child Health and Resource Development of Health and Human Services. (Peer Reviewed-1988)

I AM ONLY STAYING SIX YEARS....
AND EIGHTEEN YEARS LATER

Sonya Cruel

I am only going to stay here six years, is what I told myself as I walked in for the interview. I got to the department and Mrs. Turner was not there. She was running late. And, if you know her at all, you know she is always running. When she arrived she apologized and told me she was in a staff meeting across the street.

During the interview, we talked about things I had done at other hospitals and what my plans were long-range. She stated I know about you, your reputation preceded you. I was a little taken aback. But I put two and two together and figured my present boss had put in a good word for me. Mrs. Turner talked about the positions she had available and asked where I wanted to work. I said the outpatient oncology clinic. I figured I had worked at an inner-city outpatient clinic before, so it couldn't be that different.

It was different, in a good way. Most of the employees really cared about the patients. They saw them as family and neighbors. Some of them went way beyond the call of duty. It was a great introduction to the Grady way. I felt at home and a part of a great team of people making a difference in the lives of people others had counted out. I quickly learned that this was a calling and not just a job. I fell in love with the staff and the patients. And it was my pleasure to advocate for them regardless of who I had to go up against.

Then a position became available in Women Services. I should have walked away but I didn't. I applied for the position and became the Supervisor for the First Steps to Healthy Families
Program. These were grant-funded programs servicing families and their newborns. My skills grew as well as the programs. I became

proficient in grant writing; I traveled on Grady's dime, developed a great team, and started my education of Grady's C Suite. LAWD! The things we had to go through just to get the CEO's signature on a grant. The chain of command is long. I mean very long. I remember missing out on a grant because the CEO didn't sign on the dotted line in time. He later called me into his office and said I should never let that happen again. If I have to run him down at his car to get a signature that's what I should do.

Another promotion came and I became Manager of Women's Social Services. That included my current staff, four social workers for the Mother-Baby Unit and The Rape Crisis Center. Please note this is past my planned six years. But that was the last thing on my mind. I was enjoying the ride and I saw this as a great opportunity. This meant more interaction with the C Suite and their .... Never mind.

Leadership allows you to see a side of people. I saw who was really for the patients and workers and who was for themselves. I have to honestly say that Mrs. Turner, James Reed "JR" and Ms. Adams were committed to the social workers and the patients. They were great leaders and I learned a lot from them. I learned what Atlanta University could not teach me. I learned about teamwork, standing up for right, even if you have to stand alone. I learned about taking care of your people at all costs. I learned how to lead people who didn't necessarily like you, but you still had to support and lead for them. I learned when to speak and when not to speak. I learned how to pick my battles when it came to working with other leaders who didn't value social work. I learned if you take care of your people, your people will take care of you.

Transition is always bittersweet; it matters not if it was planned or unplanned. When Mrs. Turner and JR retired it was a hard time for me personally. It was almost like a death for me. It had nothing to do with their positions as my boss but more as a family member. They were there when my sister died, when I became guardian of my niece, they were there when I was diagnosed with breast cancer twice, they were there with my chemo and radiation appointments, they were there at major junctures of my life. And during this time our relationship changed. That was sad for me. But it was also growth for me as well.

I became Interim Director of Social Services and eventually Director. Please note, I NEVER intended to be in any leadership position at Grady. I wanted to do my six years and move on. I was well into my 13th year around this time.

Things were changing at an extremely fast rate during this time. There was a new CEO and people were coming in with limited public hospital experience. From my perspective, there seemed to be less focus on patient care. I found myself not only fighting for the social work profession but for the social workers themselves. I was coming in at 6 a.m. and leaving at 9 p.m.

The last two years were extremely hard. My staff gave me top ratings but it was not good enough. Our turnover rate was great but that was not good enough. So I decided to tap out. I turned in my resignation and told myself you have done all you can do here. It is time to move on. That was eighteen years later.

There is no place like Grady. I would not trade anything for my experiences there. I learned so much and met so many
wonderful people. People who allowed me to look over their shoulders and glean from their wealth of knowledge. People who showed me the way when I didn't know the way. I am proud of the impact I made and the impact that was made on me. I will forever be grateful to Mrs. Turner for hiring me all those many years ago. I will forever be grateful to JR for encouraging and pushing me to do more. Because of my experience at Grady, there is no hospital where I can't work and be successful.

SOCIAL WORK IS MY SECOND CAREER

V. Patricia Tatro

Social work is my second career, selected after deciding to leave the corporate world. I needed people in my life, a social career.

With my newly earned MSW, there was only one internship placement for me, Grady. Grady with the reputation of being the best place to learn medical social work. Grady Social Services lead by the renowned, Charlene Turner, LCSW, Director of Social Service.

Internships at Grady begin with, "the interview". Students interviewing at Grady would discuss among themselves how to prepare for meeting the larger than life, Ms. Turner and pass muster. We all wanted to present well, and pass muster. Dressed in my best business suit and trying to keep anxiety at bay I entered the social work office and was greeted by Ms. Turner's secretary Nancy. Anxiety eased a bit by Nancy's presence. The interview is a blur except for one crucial question Ms. Turner posed to me, "Would you like a nurturing supervisor?" Oh yes, answer to prayer.

I became an intern in Maternal Child Social Services with Estella Moore, LCSW. As an intern, Estella held me to high standards of practice while supporting my developing confidence as a social worker. Once having been rejected and sent from a patient's room for not being able to understand because "you are white" Estella sent me back to her bedside to practice social work with all assurances that I was competent.

Estella helped me to come to understand that I did not have to share someone's experience to have compassion and be of service. No, you do not have to have children to be a social worker for mothers.

Writing SOAP notes was a skill learned through the process, patiently guided by Estella, of review, discuss, ferret out the essence of what was important to document, rewrite. All handwritten as the charts at that time were paper.

Internship led to employment and I joined Estella's staff. I was assigned to cover mothers that had not received prenatal care prior to delivery. If a mother tested positive for substance use, having exposed her baby prior to delivery, a DFCS referral was mandated. Estella modeled how to be truthful, kind and compassionate, balancing relationship at the same time as making a DFCS report.

Each day at Grady offered opportunities to serve, to learn and grow personally and professionally. Once when visiting the Grady gift shop for my daily candy fix I noticed a young man pocket some candy. I confronted him and he was asked to return the candy to the shelf by the cashier who was visually impaired. As I returned to the social work office, the young man pinned me against the wall, letting me know he did not appreciate me sharing his business with anyone else. I handed him the change in my pocket and said he could go purchase the things he needed. Somehow, Ms. Turner learned of the incident and brought me into her office for a "teachable Turner moment".

HAJIB EPISODE

Taryn Siddiq

One afternoon the Social Work Department attended a Memorial Service for a former employee in the first floor Chapel for about one hour.

I had been working with a particular patient and his mother on several issues. Unbeknown to me, his mother was waiting to see me in the waiting room of the Social Services Department during the service, which is also on the first floor not far from the chapel.

After the service, we all left the chapel and most of us entered the Social Services Department waiting room where she was waiting for me.

It is important to note that I am a practicing Muslim Woman who wears the Hijab or head covering and I am a noticeable Muslim Woman on observation. My patient's mother and I have spoken in person before without any issues.

Many of my colleagues including my manager, Dollmeshia Adams, at the time were in this waiting room. As we walked in, I noticed my patient's mother was seated and I greeted her with a smile, unaware she was waiting to see me while I was in the service. She was NOT smiling, her face was RED and She appeared VERY ANGRY!!!

She yelled at me," MAYBE IF YOU WOULD TAKE THAT DAMN HEAD SCARF OFF YOU COULD LISTEN TO WHAT I NEED TO SAY TO YOU."

Well, "You could hear a pin drop!"
ALL EYES WERE ON ME!!!

I smiled and in a very calm soft voice I said, "My apologies you had to wait to see me. I would be happy to speak with you about your son and your concerns. Would you like to talk in his room or in a conference room?

I cannot remember what her choice was, as she left the waiting room. However, I do remember the gasp and sigh EVERYONE made when she left the area.

My manager said, "Taryn, you handled her and this situation very professionally. You are to be applauded. All of my colleagues agreed. They could not believe how I handled my composure.

I realized quickly I had to be professional, as a clinical social worker and represent not only our profession but My Faith. Reflecting back, I was very pleased with how I responded. I pray it modeled composure and control in a situation that could have been very ugly.

After I met with my patient's mother, she later apologized and said, "I didn't mean it. And, actually, you always look nice in your headscarves."

I cannot remember what year this took place. This is an EXPERIENCE and ENCOUNTER I will NEVER FORGET!!!

Thank You Charlene for allowing me to share this Grady Health System story/episode.

UNSUNG HEROES IN SPECIALTY AREAS

SOCIAL WORK DNA

Natasha P. Worthy

As far back as I can remember I've wanted to be a social worker. The profession was a part of my DNA with my four chemical bases being; compassion, dependability, perspective, and leadership. After graduating with my MSW from Clark Atlanta University, I was ready to save the world and was blessed to get hired at Grady Memorial Hospital as a Medical Social Worker in May 2000.

During my time there I learned a great deal about Perinatal Social Work, which is the specialization that concentrates on the concerns that emerge from pre-pregnancy through the child's first year of life (NASW 2016). The social service department at Grady was filled with professional women and men with a wealth of knowledge and who embraced and applied core social work values in their service. I was fortunate to work under the leadership of three female African American supervisors who were great examples of leadership. In this short story, I will share two memorable encounters that helped to build my DNA as a social work leader. One involves a baby taken from the hospital without being discharged.

The Mother-Baby Unit, where I was assigned, housed labor and delivery, newborn nursery, postpartum and antepartum care. My responsibilities included providing services to pregnant women hospitalized for complications, and to complete screening and assessments with mothers before discharged. As the public hospital that served the medically underserved which included but not limited to those in poverty, under or uninsured, and who were transient.

The health system's protocol required all women that delivered on the unit be seen by a social worker and complete the standard perinatal psychosocial screening and assessments. The most common psychosocial issues identified by the women served were high-risk complicated pregnancies, substance dependency, homelessness, teen pregnancy, intimate partner violence, and history of child abuse or neglect. The psychosocial screening and assessments allowed me to work with the mother to address any concerns that she may have had or discover any issues or risk factors that would indicate that it would not be safe to discharge the baby in the care of the mother.

One morning in 2002, I was making my rounds and completed a psychosocial screening and assessment on a 26-year-old African American female, who had delivered a baby boy at the hospital the night before. The mother was employed at a fast-food restaurant and had two other children. During my assessment interview with mom, I learned that she had a previous history with the county Division of Family and Children Services (DFCS) regarding her children ages 5 and 3. Mom shared with me that she had a stable place to live, that she had a car seat and items for the baby, and a support system of family and friends to assist her if needed. I shared with the mom that I appreciated her honesty about her DFCS history and that it was the hospital's policy that we contact DFCS regarding previous cases to ensure that there weren't any current cases open and that it would be safe to discharge newborns in their mother's care. She stated that she understood and that she had no questions.

After contacting the local DFCS office I learned that the patient's 5 and 3-year-old were not in her custody due to child abuse and neglect and that the case was still under investigation. The DFCS caseworker in charge of her case notified me that she was coming to the hospital to see mom and that we were not to release the baby in mom's care. I informed the charge nurse to delay the mom's discharge and wrote my notes in the chart that the DFCS worker would be by the following day to interview mom. Later that day while in my office I heard an alarm and ran to the floor to see what was going on, only to learn that my patient had taken her baby out of the hospital. A nurse had taken the baby in to visit with mom and while there, mom somehow took off the baby's monitoring device from his ankle.

Needless to say, I was shocked and was replaying my encounter with the patient over and over in my head. My supervisor, Delbra Thomas came to the floor to discuss the case and I shared with her my interaction with mom. She confirmed that I followed protocol and accompanied me during my interview with the police detectives on the case. I thanked God she did!!! Although the detectives were doing their jobs, their questioning was a bit accusatory and harsh at times. I am thankful that Delbra was there because after 45 minutes or more of answering the same questions, and providing the same answers, it became a bit overwhelming.

Delbra calmly informed the detectives that I followed protocol and that this incident had also been distressing for me as well. Basically, she let them know that enough was enough, and reassured them that I was willing to cooperate in any way possible, which led them to end the interview.

We returned to my office where we debriefed about the event. Delbra's leadership and support during that ordeal helped me to build upon and strengthen my DNA as a social worker. She modeled for me empathy, trust, and dependability, courage, and influence. The mere fact that she accompanied me in the interview with the detectives and did not let me face that situation alone as a rookie social worker modeled empathy. She shared that she could imagine herself in my position and understood the possible range of emotions and thoughts that I was experiencing at that time. From the initial moment when I met with Delbra, after the baby was taken and I explained to her what happened, she was supportive. She never made me doubt my actions with handling this case or showed concern of foul play on my part. Her support and leadership throughout the entire ordeal demonstrated teamwork, although she was my supervisor, I felt that we were in it together. Which as a result fostered trust because she was there when I needed her. I was in a vulnerable situation and her actions displayed her genuine concern for me and proved that she was dependable.

In addition, to modeling trust and dependability, she modeled courage. I was amazed at how she persuasively communicated to the detectives that it was time to end the interview. I know I was not expecting that pivot and based on the look on the detective's faces they weren't either, nevertheless, they did let me go. Delbra's courageous act showed that she was able to push through uncomfortable situations and did not back down when things got hard. The final quality she displayed was influence. Her leadership during this situation gained my admiration and inspired in me the desire to develop into such a leader, who would have a positive influence on other social workers as she had on me.

So, I guess you are wondering what happened with the case? The following day the police found both the mom and the baby at a relative's home. The patient stated that she was afraid that DFCS was going to take her baby, so she devised a plan with one of her relatives to take the child from the hospital. She stated that she became suspicious when her discharge date was moved back and because she knew she was not honest with me about her other children.

Fortunately, this story had a happy ending. The baby was returned safely back to the hospital and I continued to store leadership information which helped to build and sustain my DNA as a social work leader.

RESILIENCE

Phyllis A. Sanders

The strengths that people and systems demonstrate that enable them to rise above adversity (Van Breda, 2001).

I remember my first day at Grady. It was actually my job interview with Charlene Turner, Director of Social Services. I had not yet graduated from the Atlanta University School of Social Work and was dressed for a graduation event that very day. The interview and the event were so close in time that I did not have time to change from one appointment to the next. I felt so uncomfortable as I was not dressed as professionally as I felt I should have been for the job interview. I had on what I thought was a cute black dress that I was going to wear under my graduation gown. I apologized profusely, completed the interview, and thanked Charlene for the opportunity. Despite my dress, I did get the job thankfully and worked at Grady for ten years.

I started out working on the Neurology floor with medical patients and moved quickly to Psychiatry, where I worked at the Psychiatric Day Treatment Program. It was there that I learned one of my first clinical social work lessons that is now viewed as a norm, inter-disciplinary teamwork. I remember it was Dr. Garret that pulled the team together every morning to review cases, (psychiatrist, psychiatric nurse, psychiatric intern, psychiatric social worker, occupational therapist, recreational therapist, etc.) to create, review and revise treatment plans. Of course, this sounds run of the mill now, but it was quite groundbreaking at the time.

I also remember having an office where the coffee pot sat outside of my door and patients walked back and forth all day getting hot coffee even when it was 80-90 degrees outside. I know now, what I did not know then, coffee may boost the production of dopamine and serotonin, the hormones that reduce anxiety and stress levels. I also had my first experience with a patient with tardive dyskinesia, as there were no Selective Serotonin Reuptake Inhibitors (SSRIs) at that time and patients often had horrible reactions to being on long term psychotropic medications. There was one patient at the day treatment center who was painful to watch as he struggled all day with grunts and groans trying to contain his involuntary movements due to tardive dyskinesia.

My love, however, was working in Child Psychiatry. It was located in what I was told was a former nurse's dorm-Georgia Hall. This was an old house that had been repurposed for various uses throughout the years. I loved this place. It was a little sanctuary down the street from the "Big Grady" for the children and their families. Every day when I walked to Georgia Hall, I had a little pep in my step because I loved the work so much. It was not just the work it was everything-the children, their parents, the staff (housekeeper, receptionist, secretaries, therapists, and doctors), the environment itself. I say the environment itself because initially, the building was beige and not very colorful, but we (the staff) decided to take a Saturday and paint the clinic to brighten the environment for the children. It had what I remembered as a long staircase and you could see everyone coming down into the clinic. I can still picture the green and blue stripes that made all the difference in the world. It was something about this clinic that no matter who you came in contact with, you felt a sincere warmth. I would dare say a feeling of love. (I still to this day cherish a small book of memories that the staff gave me when I left the clinic after many years of work there.)

It is here that I learned one of my most important lessons of resilience. I worked with young people who primarily came from environments with meager incomes and often very disadvantaged circumstances. I remember working with a young male whose mother had mental health issues. This young person came to the clinic on a regular basis and seemed to benefit from the consistent support, as he experienced very inconsistent parenting. It was amazing to me at that time how he managed to move through life in such "a normal way" with little to no structure at home. He in fact appeared to be rearing himself. I met with him regularly and learned that though life may present you with little advantages, it does not mean that you cannot take what is given and make the most of it.

Then there was the young female that was assaulted and had to drag her way to safety to obtain help. She always had a beautiful smile and worked through this traumatic event with her therapist. Having limited experience, I learned that most children were abused by someone they knew who had gained their confidence. Many times, it was a close family member. I learned as a therapist that one of the most important things I could do was to help abused children understand that the abuse was not their fault.

I observed as children drew, played games, and acted out their feelings with puppets. They worked through thoughts to often help them resolve life traumas. Frequently in their pictures, they would start out with dark themes emerging into brighter colors. I learned that you did not always have to verbalize your feelings to make positive changes in thought patterns.

I also learned that sometimes I could over-analyze things. I remember the young child that presented as extremely sad and would not interact with other children. Of course, an array of clinical interventions came to mind when I first started working with this young person. Someone on staff, however, realized that she really wanted to just look like the other children in her class. When we brought in some new dresses for her things changed. Subsequently, she exhibited a happy demeanor and appeared to easily interact with others. The issue was resolved and had been staring me in the face all along. Of course, most cases did not resolve this easily.

There were challenges. I soon learned there are times that no matter how hard you try, you cannot protect a person from themselves. If someone is intent on harming themselves, they may find a way. Sadly, one of my adolescent patients took their life. I completed an assessment with a young person and connected then with one of the center's psychiatrist. However, before we could truly begin work, I learned this young person took their life. Of course, being a young therapist, I questioned whether there was more that I could have done. I was plagued by this question for many years. I also learned that it is important for a therapist to have clinical supervision for case review but also to honestly process feelings about their clinical work. Without reliving the case here, I will say it was a very painful process and one of the hardest clinical social work lessons I learned.

I learned as a therapist that connection is the most important part of the therapeutic relationship. Without it, there is truly little that can be done.

During the course of my now over thirty years of social work (administrative and clinical), there are very few positions that I would want to repeat. If I could time travel, my work in Child Psychiatry in Georgia Hall with the same staff would be one that I would revisit. The rewards and challenges were great! The resilience of the children and their families was immense.

The lessons learned were priceless!!!

TALES FROM THE GRADY SURGICAL INTENSIVE CARE UNIT

Nancy Moore

For five years I worked in the Surgical Intensive Care Unit (SICU) as a medical social worker. The SICU is a place where most of the patients are intubated and sedated; a place where when patients are taken off the vent and actually able to talk, it is a sign that they are ready to be transferred to a lower level of care; a place where patients' families stay for days and weeks at a time, unwilling to leave, while their loved ones are so critically ill. These are some of their stories.

As Grady is the largest Level 1 Trauma Center in the region, trauma patients are brought there from all over. The vast majority of them started the day with no idea whatsoever that it would end in admission to Grady. Some of them had never even heard of Grady before their admission there. Some would arrive with little or no identification or no information about next of kin. My initial job always with these patients was to identify them and to locate and contact next of kin.

One such patient was a middle-aged white male who lived well north of Atlanta. He was driving to visit family in a neighboring state when he was critically injured in a major car crash. He was picked up by air ambulance and brought to Grady's rooftop heliport. After being intubated and sedated he was admitted to the SICU. The only information on him was a card from an out of state medical center identifying him by name as a kidney transplant recipient. I called that medical center and spoke with someone in the transplant department, describing what had happened and asking for any information available about next of kin. I was told that they would attempt to notify the family and ask them to call me. Within 20 minutes the patient's mother called. She said that the family had been frantically searching for him. When he did not arrive at his destination, his brother had driven the entire route the patient would have taken. Of course, the car wreckage had been totally cleared long before he arrived. And, since Grady was nowhere along that route, it hadn't even crossed their minds to call there. After that call with his mother, the patient's family was in his room with him as soon as it was humanly possible for them to arrive.

As this patient and his family made abundantly clear, most times if we had not been able to locate family, that family was searching for the patient, using all the resources at their disposal to locate their missing loved one. Thus, it was imperative that we prioritize reuniting patients and their families.

A white male in his twenties was admitted with head injuries following a motorcycle accident. He was intubated and sedated. His partner was constantly in his room to provide support. Eventually, the sedation was decreased, and the patient became more aware of his surroundings. He began to follow commands —putting up two or three fingers when asked. Since he was still on the ventilator, he could not talk; since he had a head injury, his cognitive abilities were unknown. His partner reported that he had begun to make random hand movements and was becoming increasingly agitated as he did so. Members of his medical team observed the same behavior. This went on for several days until, finally, someone said, "He's signing!" His hand movements were sign language, which no one recognized; his agitation was frustration at not being able to make anyone understand.

A sign language interpreter came to the room, and the patient began to communicate. Not only did the patient have a skill-sign language- which no one knew he had, he also demonstrated that his cognitive abilities were intact.

An African American college student was admitted after being hit by a car while he was crossing a street on campus. His injuries were so severe; his prognosis was so poor that he was not expected to live. He was the only child of his single-parent father, a social worker who provided community outreach services for a local social service agency. There was just something about this young man that touched me deeply. Maybe it was the randomness of it—just another day going to class when suddenly, out of nowhere, his life was changed forever. But, then, the SICU beds were filled with people whose lives had been changed in an instant. Maybe it was the fact that his father was a social worker, but, really, it was this patient himself to whom I was drawn. For whatever reason I felt compelled to pray, to really pray for him. Every time I went by his room, I said a prayer for him. Eventually, the prayers began shorter and more urgent, basically asking God to not only save his life but to restore him to his previous functioning. In all the weeks he was in the SICU we never had a conversation, nor did as much as a greeting pass between us—he was intubated and sedated. I did, of course, keep in touch with his father. Over time, the patient did improve and was transferred to a lower level of care.

I lost track of him but still kept praying for him. One day about 10 months later when I arrived on the unit, the clerk told me that a young man had been there to see me. Since I wasn't there, he had left a note for me. The note was a beautiful handwritten thank you note. Did you get that? Less than one year after this young man was expected to die, he walked into the SICU and delivered a note he had written! Now that truly was a miracle flowing from the power of prayer and from the power of excellent medical care.

HIV/AIDS SOCIAL WORK AT GRADY

Dorothy Ziemer

Several years ago, my mother called to tell me that one of my cousins had died. "Everybody knew he was queer," she offered in her less than tactful manner. "But, if any child of mine died in his 30's, there would be an autopsy - you don't die from being queer."

A few months later, The Morbidity and Mortality Weekly Report (MMWR) prepared by the Centers for Disease Control and Prevention (CDC) reported on the new "gay" disease.

Eight years later, I became one of two "AIDS Social Workers" at Grady. I thought I knew something about HIV/AIDS - after all, I had been an AIDS Social Worker.

Grady was different – the only similarity was an outpatient clinic half-day a week. The clinic at Grady saw people every day in a very small space.

The hospital had more than twenty units. Most of the general medicine and surgery units had two four-bed wards, one eight-bed ward, and nine semi-private rooms. Also, there were sixteen medical teams, plus ICU teams and surgical teams. Admissions were handwritten in ledger books on each unit. Admissions from the emergency room were handwritten in large notebooks.

In order to identify and see people hospitalized with HIV/AIDS, I checked on admissions from the clinic, then reviewed the emergency room logs, then walked from floor to floor. As I moved from place to place, I saw them, if possible, wrote the note and kept moving. The head of Emory Medicine at Grady was an advocate for our folks, so there was an expectation that they would be treated with respect. That was not always the case, however.

Treatment and resources for aftercare were limited; so many people with HIV/AIDS remained hospitalized for prolonged periods. This often put Social Workers in a position where physicians, Utilization Managers, sometimes nursing staff wanted people out of the hospital but there were few places for them to go. Even when people had family or friends willing to care for them, it was often more than a full-time job.

One of my first assignments was a quiet young man who had been at GMH for months; he had no family and there were no personal care homes or nursing homes that would accept him. He could care for himself, but could not live alone. He had friends who had been trying to find a place where he could be fed and safe.

An older man who was caring for another family member offered a room in his home – we went to meet him and see his home. It was a modest home, but clean and well kept. He was delighted at the idea of his own room, not in a hospital. His friends helped him move and continued their support for the rest of his life there.

The following year, we were able to move an older man who had no family to a personal care home. He was a thin man, looking older than his years, who took pride in his being a hard worker. He was independent and had been able to take care of himself. He came to the hospital only as a last resort. He was diagnosed with HIV and pneumocystis pneumonia, PCP, which equaled a diagnosis of AIDS. He was devastated and frightened about his future. One of our social work interns spent the day calling every personal care home in town. She pleaded and educated. She was able to convince a former nurse at Grady who had a personal care home to take him in. Until she closed her personal care home in 2016, she remained a strong advocate for our folks with other personal care homeowners, helping to open doors for many more people.

In 1991, two more social workers were hired to deal with the inpatient population — which had doubled from around eighty admissions a month.

Other people who had long hospital stays were not as lucky. Many were bed-bound and it was not until 1992 that — after many meetings and negotiations — we successfully admitted one of our gentlemen to a nursing home. He was an older man whose sister was a nurse at Grady. He was quiet, pleasant, and not very mobile — all went well, so we had a second man admitted. He was much younger and more mobile; he had spent months in an eight-bed ward and had become a helper to his roommates — he would go to the snack machine, make calls on the payphone, communicate with staff. All of this was appreciated and seen as helpful.

When he arrived at the nursing home, he attempted to do the same, but there he was seen as a threat. Nursing home staff and residents were upset because he was going into other residents' rooms — he was returned to Grady; Grady returned him to the nursing home who refused to accept him and the EMS staff were circling around trying to figure out what to do. By this time, he was confused and angry.

Finally, he was admitted to Psychiatry to be cleared, while other housing arrangements could be made. Of course, this happened on a Friday afternoon — a prime time for crises, real or imagined. Subsequently, nursing home criteria focused on mobility — those who were walking around could go to personal care homes. Shelters were a good resource for some people — in some cases, shelter staff provided needed services for a resident who might have been with them for years.

And there was the Atlantan Hotel — where we could send those folks who needed some stability but were not appropriate for either a nursing home, personal care home or shelter. Often these were people who were transgender or had some special need, such as being wheelchair-bound.

I met one of our transgender folks when she was newly diagnosed. Despite her looking very feminine – to the extent that one of the doctors in the emergency room had tried to do a pelvic exam - and having a female name, she was in a four-bed ward with three men. This arrangement was confusing to her roommates, staff, and doctors, some of whom insisted on referring to her as a man.

She was personable and chatty – the diagnosis was less of an issue than where would she live, how would she make ends meet. She also met the diagnosis for AIDS and therefore a disability application was taken. Upon discharge, she was sent to the Atlantan Hotel to recuperate.

When her disability did not come as quickly as it should have – there was a way to get cases expedited – she came to see me. Turned out the check had come to the hotel in her given name and since no one knew her by that name, the check had been returned to Social Security. Her claim was on the way to being closed out as lost. She was a good advocate for herself.

Grady Hospice was available as a resource to provide support to people whose families were willing and able to have them at home. However, many of our people either had no family or were estranged from them. Atlanta was the big city for the Southeastern US, so many of our folks had come here from rural or small towns, seeking a better life or a place where they could be themselves.

Finding family was a challenge as these were the days before the internet – we would call Information Operators to see if there was a Mary Smith listed in wherever; then spend time calling all the people with that name in an effort to locate family. Despite the general belief that families were uncaring, I found that most families – if we could find them - were supportive once they had information and resources.

Often when the family was located we were told they had been looking for the ill family member for years/months – driving through areas where homeless people stayed, scouring hospitals and jails for some clue as to where they might be.

Family members would come by car, bus or plane – from across town and across the country to and in some cases across the ocean to spend time with a family member.

Nursing staff asked me to see a fellow who was admitted; he requested that I 'go get his stuff' from the Salvation Army where he had been prior to admission. I told him we could call them and see what could be arranged. He dismissed me as being of no use.

A week or two later, he was readmitted. Two social work assistants interviewed new admissions to gather information on their next of kin and/or emergency contact. When he was approached with this question, he told the employee he had no one; she persisted and he proceeded to get loud and tell her to leave. She told me about her encounter and with reluctance, I returned to see him. Surprisingly, he was calm and wanted to apologize to her. This was the beginning of a relationship that lasted for years. He told me he had questioned why he became so upset at her questions; he did want to reach out to his family but feared rejection. He had been to the library to scour phone books and city directories to find family; he had written a letter but not sent it. Though he had HIV/AIDS, he had other medical conditions that brought him into the hospital often. He would talk about his ambivalence and at last, he sent the letter.

Shortly after that, he decided to move to San Francisco –saying that he did not care if he located his family; he could make it on his own. He planned to move into a single room occupancy and when he became too ill to care for himself, he was going to pay 'some drunks' to take him down to the bay, and go out with the tide and thus no longer be anyone's problem.

He moved to San Francisco and shortly after he left, I got a call from an old friend of his from home – he had received the letter and been trying to track him down. I told him what I knew. There was no listing for him in San Francisco – so the matter seemed closed – his friend could check.

A year or so later, when I had a few minutes to go through the mass of paper that accumulated on my desk, I came across the message from his friend – I tried information again – and there was a number! I called – he recognized my voice and reported he had an apartment, was working for an AIDS organization – had friends! The move was a success. When I told him I had heard from his friend, he became quiet. He wanted to think about it. I gave him his friend's number and again considered the matter closed.

Still more years later, he called to ask me to help him secure oxygen locally for a conference – something I could actually do fairly easily then. During his stay, he stopped by Grady, told me he had been in touch with his family and friends back home.

Subsequently, he did return home where his family was accepting and caring. Jane and John Doe's were also an issue. One young woman who had been brought in and had died was known on the street by a nickname; one of our street team partners returned to the area where she had been picked up. She was able to give us a first name by talking to the other folks in that area.

Using detective skills as well as social work skills, we checked on all the folks with that first name. Fortunately, it was not a really common name. All but one was accounted for and when we spoke to her family, we were told they had not seen her for about two weeks – the length of time she had been hospitalized. Our Jane Doe was identified.

The internet, Facebook and other social media have taken the place of the phone book. Locating family is not easier, just different because when people want to get lost, they can. However, even when the news is not good, closure can be important to all involved – the family and the person with HIV/AIDS. Time and energy spent on locating family was worthwhile.

Haven House opened in 1992; it was a hospice program that provided a place to live and round the clock care for people who met the criteria for hospice – that they would die within six months. Since treatment for HIV/AIDS was limited – many people qualified. And it met the need for those people who had no one. There were people who went to Haven House, where the love and care they received allowed them to improve – to 'graduate' from hospice.

One former problem placement went on to get both a Bachelor's and a Master's degree; another was able to enjoy playing golf. This was a time before antiretrovirals. Everyone did not have the miracle experience, yet their death was peaceful and they were surrounded by people who loved them.

In 1993, two more staff were hired and admissions were 200 or more a month. Resources and treatment existed though both were limited. Gift of Grace, a home for women with HIV/AIDS, opened in 1994. It is run by the Missionaries of Charity – Mother- now Saint- Teresa's order. They started as a hospice, but have changed with the times, like many other housing programs. The nuns provide a home to women with HIV/AIDS who have no other options. For many women, it provided a community of acceptance. Similar to Haven House, residents come in weak and frail and regain independence. Several of the women come in unable to manage for themselves and leave, independent, with housing and jobs. Many of them returned to volunteer and offer hope and care to others.

In 1996, treatment became more effective and allowed people with HIV/AIDS to live; the number of deaths in 1995 was more than 900 and in 1996, the number dropped to 600 and has continued to drop since then; when I retired in 2017, there were less than 200 deaths – and the numbers continue to drop.

Services changed from providing comfort and support to encouraging people to get into care and to manage their disease. Inpatient numbers have dropped as well, although there are still probably more admissions at Grady than other hospitals have; there is no longer a dedicated team of social workers to follow those with HIV/AIDS. While treatment is not a cure, it has allowed people to get on with their lives.

MAKING A CASE FOR ADVOCACY: OPPORTUNITIES FOR GROWTH AND GREATNESS

Patti Hammonds-Greene

I was the burn unit social worker for the Grady Burn Center from 2001-2008. As the burn unit social worker, I was responsible for providing social work case management services to patients and to families in the burn intensive care unit, the burn step-down unit, and the burn clinic. Grady's Regional Burn Center received patients from all over the state and bordering states.

This dynamic transformational experience allowed me to engage in micro, mezzo, and macro levels of social work practice. My practice was and still is guided by our social work core competencies. Many days I was educating frightened patients and families about burn care, the burn unit, and its processes and procedures. I provided emotional, crisis, and resource support to patients and families. In addition, I documented treatment plans and interventions in the charts, attended family conferences and multidisciplinary rounds, and attempted to evade all staff meetings. Many times, I assisted families with lodging, meals, and transportation. I had many "spirited" conversations with child protection service agencies concerning the safe disposition of many pediatric burn patients. When insurance companies would deny clinically indicated and physician-recommended services for patients, I would aggressively work with patients and families to appeal the insurance denials.

Many of the patients admitted to the burn center were uninsured or underinsured. As the social worker, I would contact vendors, partners, and other community stakeholders and ask them to provide charity care services to our patients and families. On some occasions, I would facilitate pediatric transfers to other specialized facilities. This included a lot of communication and coordination with patients, families, and the accepting facilities. In addition, I was involved in a few medical repatriation cases where patients were sent back to their country of origin to continue their medical care and to be with their extended families for discharge support. These specialized types of transfers were tedious and involved many "moving parts" and allowed me to interact with numerous agencies. Also, I wrote many letters to the Georgia State Legislature to support the expansion of trauma care funding in the state, specifically to Grady Health System.

When I think about the culmination of my experiences as the burn unit social worker at Grady Health System, I am reminded of the intersectionality of healthcare and social issues and also of the rich history of medical social work practice. Medical social work practice is rooted in agitation, advocacy, and accountability. During my tenure as the burn unit social worker, most of my interventions, engagements, conversations, and actions centered around solution-focused advocacy. This bias towards action was contagious because many times it resulted in the entire burn team working with me to bring about a solution for injustice against our patient.

As I continue to reflect on my time as the burn unit social worker, I was well respected, valued, and always encouraged to practice autonomously. There was a mutual respect for all disciplines on the burn team.

However, some of my colleagues on other areas struggled to maintain their professional integrity. This was especially true at the time the departmental structure was realigned to meet the requirements of new leadership and /or outside consultants. From my standpoint as a staff social worker, this was a period when our worth and skillsets were challenged. This is why advocacy is so vital to our practice because many times we have to advocate for ourselves before we can advocate for anyone else.

As social workers, we must terminate all deodorized discussions with others attempting to define us and to tell us what we should do. We must never allow anyone, under any circumstances, "to inoculate us for their convenience." Instead, we must establish our own voices in the current social work scholarship. We must amplify our conversation of advocacy which should result in action-oriented, solution-focused and progressive social work practice. Social workers understand people, pedagogy, policies, practices, processes, and systems. We must find a way to capitalize on our many skills by quantifying our results and outcomes in real-time. We are the problem-solvers on the team and we cannot afford to live in "I don't know", "I don't know how" or "that is not my patient" because these temporary spaces retard professional growth and breed mediocrity.

More now than ever and especially in this pandemic, medical social workers must continue to answer our phones, respond to e-mails, and return calls when no one else does. We must continue to work our cases, broker and mobilize resources, and be willing to accept a 100 "no's" to get a "yes." We must challenge systems and processes to solve complex problems. Our interventions are deliberate, intentional, methodical, and should ultimately move the case towards a targeted solution. While working as a social worker on the burn unit, I learned the true value of social work practice and how the profession tends to shift the culture and atmosphere of an environment for the patients, families, and even the employees. I have carried the lessons from the burn unit as I continue to work in healthcare during this COVID-19 pandemic. Although social workers have been exempt from many "front line" worker discussions, our presence has been impactful and has made a positive difference in the lives of many patients and families. I realize that because the pace of societal change shows no sign of slackening, social workers of the 21st century must become adept problem solvers and be able to wrestle with ill-defined social problems and win. Problem-solving is the cognitive passport of the future. Social work practice focused primarily on content acquisition and theory does not prepare us to successfully engage an increasingly complex world.

Our pedagogy, knowledge, skills, and practice must result in outcomes and solutions for our patients and families.

While working for my patients and families on the burn unit, I developed a "focused advocacy" mindset. I attributed my success of overturning insurance denials, mobilizing resources for patients, and getting unfunded patients placed to this mentality. This mindset calls for social workers to practice from a revolutionary and victorious space. This clarion call challenges social workers to infect their patients and families with a sense of urgency as it relates to their motivation to change.

This mindset calls for medical social workers to lose the need for explicit permission before taking a calculated risky action. It is a mindset that empowers social workers to make decisions as part of their regular professional practice. It is a mindset that cultivates courageous and critical thinking problem-solvers.

When your patients are denied services, continue to advocate. When you are told that your patient cannot return to a facility, elevate your advocacy to the highest level in the facility. When others think they can do your job, stay focused, and demonstrate what you can do. When non-social work consultants enter your space, it is time to educate. When the doctors and other members of your team disagree with your analysis, continue to speak your truth in the best interest of your patients. Social work colleagues, when you embrace this brand of advocacy, your practice improves and new criteria for life emerges.

LIFE IN THE DAY OF A GRADY SOCIAL WORKER

Valeria Beasley

My journey in the Social Work profession at Grady is quite unique and different than my colleagues. I started as a Social Worker Assistant. Initially, I was responsible for contacting family members of unidentified patients often by utilizing the Police Department to have patients fingerprinted to help with identifying them.

Through the urging of my Director, Charlene Turner (in whom I was often in conflict), I decided to go back to school to obtain my Bachelor's Degree. Ms. Turner also encouraged me to keep going to obtain my Master's Degree, however, I did not listen to her. Years later after Ms. Turner's retirement, I decided to go back and obtain my MSW, not knowing that our paths would cross again in the social work arena. I have grown to appreciate, admire, and respect Ms. Turner as a friend and social worker. I am grateful that she thought enough of me to include me in being a part of this book.

Holiday Food Drive

For over 10 years, I was the social worker for the Medical Clinic. Every Christmas we would have a holiday food drive. I spearheaded the food drive where we would raise money from staff in the Medical Clinic; we also collected can goods to distribute to patients. I would raise approximately $4,000.00 - $5,000.00 every year. Mind you, this was back in 1986-1996, you could do a lot of shopping back then. I worked closely with the Medical Director in the clinic and we had the doctors to go shopping. The food drive was primarily for our elderly patients who suffered from food insecurity. Staff in the Medical Clinic participated in collecting and packing boxes, delivering food to patients and shopping. We would go out in teams to deliver the food, the teams consisted of someone from the Metro Atlanta area along with the

physicians in clinics. We had physicians from different states and countries that participated in the delivery of over 200 food boxes. This turned out to be a true learning experience
for the physicians.

One physician asked if we would be able to get in the security gates, not realizing that Grady was a public hospital located in the middle of downtown area, surrounded by low-income government-subsidized housing in the ghetto (hood).

This was in 1986, security gates had not been heard of for these apartments. We went to a home in the Vine City area where people were in the house using drugs, another couple was having sex in the other room. Going to Thomasville Heights, was enlightening because you had a group of young boys controlling who came in and out of the neighborhood. They would stop you upon entering the parking lot to ask the apartment number before you were allowed to enter.

Some of the things the physicians learned from the food drive were:
- There was a better understanding of why a lot of their patients were alcoholics. When they visited patient neighborhoods, they realized that there was a package store (liquor store) on every corner.
- They got a chance to see how far their patients had to walk to the bus stop. And, that if they missed a bus, how long they would have to wait for the next one. So, they could better understand their patients being late for their appointments.
- They saw that there were no major grocery stores in their patients' neighborhoods. They learned that patients had to purchase food from convenience stores or local supermarkets, which were more expensive and had no fresh meat or vegetables.
- They saw elderly patients using their stoves and ovens to heat their apartments to keep from running up their heating bill.

Addendum:

Ms. Beasley deserves special commendation for organizing and coordinating this food drive which became an annual event. It represented a great example of teamwork par excellence -social workers, clerks, nurses, and, of course, the doctors in the medical clinic who bankrolled the event. It represented not only outreach to the community —but it demonstrated to patients how much the staff at Grady cared about them as people.

This effort, along with Ms. Beasley's commitment to working with her patients earned her special recognition from her medical and nursing staff. On more than one occasion when I was called upon to educate the doctors about social work issues and/or resources, doctors would interrupt me and proudly proclaim that they never had to deal with such issues as they had Ms. Beasley who handled these cases for them. And, many of them would routinely tell me that she covered so many cases and needed another social worker to help her.

Charlene Turner

GERIATRIC CLINIC

Louise Spiro

I was the first employee of the Grady Geriatric Clinic in 1998. Two rooms in the Medical Clinic were set aside for the new Geriatric clinic and Dr. Michael Lubin and myself were staffed to run it. Since the clinic was only open 2 half days a week upon opening, I was a Medical Clinic Social worker for the remainder of the week. The first room was my office and when the Geriatric clinic was operating, it became the room in which Dr. Lubin, one to two residents as well as myself stayed. It became very crowded and noisy as patients were discussed and decisions were made. The second room was where the patient was seen. This was quite a problem. When clinic began, Dr. Lubin would come into the room and immediately, clear my desk with one arm, sit at the desk announcing that he was ready for clinic. With each new patient, he would ask me to inform them that "Geriatric is for real." Medical clinic never seemed to understand that the social worker was not doing Medical clinic when Geriatric was in session. I would continue to have knocks on the door from Medical Clinic patients wanting to see the social worker. I would direct them to the other social worker or asked them to come back at another time.

About six months after the clinic had opened, I was told that Grady had hired a Geriatrician who was to start soon. The same day turned into a practically busy day with many demands from the Geriatric Doctors and many knocks at the door from Medical Clinic patients. As I became a little flustered, there was one more knock at the door and when I answered it, I asked, "and what do you want?" rather abruptly. There stood a very tall man with shoulder-length hair wearing blue jeans. He smiled broadly and replied that he was, "Dr. Jonathan Flacker, I'm the new Geriatrician. "Needless to say, I was very embarrassed and Dr. Flacker never let me forget this meeting. Despite this, we became a very efficient and well-run team that eventually got our own space developed with our needs in mind as we became a full-time clinic.

One of the things that both Dr. Flacker and I agreed upon was how difficult it was for bedbound patients to receive needed medical care. They would arrive via stretcher, wait in the hall for hours to be seen by the doctor for maybe 15 minutes and then wait more hours for transportation to get them and return them to their home. Dr. Flacker and I developed a plan where Dr. Flacker would do home visits for the bedbound patients once a month. As the social worker, I help pick the patients that would best benefit from this program. I then made all the arrangements; was certain we had the needed equipment required by the doctor as well as the paperwork needed for orders and documentation. I would document the visit and provide social worker services.

Each month, I would take Dr. Flacker in my car and drive him to the various homes to visit. He would joke that the reason I was hired was because I knew the city so well. I could tell him by the address what kind of neighborhood we were going to so he would not be surprised. One day, I didn't come to work and Dr. Flacker decided he could go on a home visit without the social worker. The next day, when I returned to work, I asked him how things went on his visit. He said it was very strange. When he arrived, there was a house filled with people who left when he entered but waited outside until he left. They then went back into the house. I laughed and told him that it was a crack house he had visited. I always cleared out the house before he came and made sure only the patient and her caregiver were present. Dr. Flacker never went on a home visit without the social worker again.

EXPERIENCES WITH PEDIATRIC SERVICES

Judy Martin Plecko

It was 1972 when I was hired to be the Chief Social Worker in Pediatrics at Grady. I was 24 years old and had just held one other social work position since I finished graduate school at the University of Texas. That position was as the "lone social worker" and hence, the Social Work Director at Elks Aidemore Hospital in Atlanta.

Aidemore was a private non-profit children's hospital with 42 long term beds. It was located on the campus of Emory University where I had attended undergraduate school. It was "attached to Egleston Hospital, which was the pediatric training hospital for Emory Medical School.

Many of the children at Aidemore were there because they couldn't receive adequate care post-discharge at home. Some were in foster care and others were orthopedic patients, who were essentially bed bound for long periods. Some had chronic conditions like sickle cell or birth defects, but none were terminal.

The social work department structure at Grady in 1972, allowed for 2 pediatric social work positions. The "chief" covered all the outpatient specialty clinics and the pediatric emergency and appointment clinics and a social worker covered the inpatient units. The volume of patients seen was overwhelming. The physician who was the Chief of Pediatrics had reportedly not been pleased with the social workers who had served his department previously. He was feared by medical students, interns, and residents alike. I recognized that social workers were "guests" in the large medical and teaching hospital system, which was designed for a different purpose and had its own bureaucracy and expectations. I knew I would have to deal with systemic challenges, as well as those encountered dealing with children and their families.

The referrals came to me for all the outpatient clinics. I needed to prioritize and be responsive. Since the pediatric interns and residents rotated through the clinics at different times, I knew that I'd need to maintain contact about referrals with the faculty member who was in charge of each specialty service. Many times, I became the main link for families to deal with a system that I had to quickly learn myself. The clinics included Cystic Fibrosis, Neurology, Gastroenterology, Arthritis, Allergy, and Hematology/Tumor. The general pediatric clinic was called the PAC or Pediatric Appointment Clinic, which actually served as a point of entry to the specialty clinics. The pediatric emergency clinic (PEC) was high volume and needed immediate follow-up, because potential child abuse and neglect cases would be referred.

The Hematology and Tumor clinic patients included those children diagnosed with Sickle Cell Anemia, Leukemia, and various types of cancer tumors. Many of these children would need to be seen regularly. The faculty doctor in charge of that clinic recognized that these families needed multiple sources of support and these children required frequent hospitalizations as well. I could maintain contact with parents and children during all these treatments.

One particular child and family is still in my heart. TJ was about 2 years old when she was diagnosed with a brain tumor. It was a glioblastoma and was inoperable at the time. Some treatments were done, but sadly, the diagnosis was a terminal one. TJ was a lively and engaging African American child, who was always smiling. Her father worked but came to some appointments. Her 2 older brothers were in school but came on weekends when she was hospitalized.

Over several months, I became close to this child and her family. Her mother called me frequently to talk and I was usually present at her outpatient clinic appointments. Her mother asked me to check on her when she was hospitalized, especially, if she couldn't be there at times. I would visit her daily.

Initially, TJ would play with me and talk, even if she had IV's or seemed drowsy. Her symptoms, including some paralysis, began to overtake her, so efforts became geared to keeping her comfortable. She slowly drifted into an unconscious state but didn't appear to be in pain. Her mother kept her favorite stuffed animals with her in her bed.

One morning, I came to work to find out that she had died during the night. I saw her family when they came in to see her. They were planning the funeral at their Baptist Church and invited me to attend. When I got all the information, I wasn't sure if I could handle going. I had been to several funerals, but not an African American one and not a child's funeral. It was also being held in a part of Atlanta, unknown to me. I never thought about the fact that this might be an "unusual" action for a young white social worker.

I decided to go to honor that sweet child and her family. There was an open casket and TJ's favorite stuffed animals were with her, as well as many additional ones around the casket. My tears came freely. After the service, when her family saw me, they hugged me and thanked me for coming and being so special to TJ and to them. The mother later sent me a beautiful thank you note. Those moments have stayed with me for almost 50 years.

A UNIQUE GROUP EXPERIENCE

Charlene Turner

Mr. W walked into my office one Friday afternoon and explained in a very agitated state that he had just received an AIDS diagnosis. He explained that he was all alone and wanted a guarantee that he would have a decent burial. After considerable discussion, he appeared to be calmer and did not appear to be a suicide risk. He denied having any thought of killing himself or anyone else and refused any suggestions to speak with someone in Psychiatry. He would not provide contact information for his family, but he did give his telephone number and address. I attempted to reach him over the weekend, but my calls went unanswered. To my great dismay, on Monday, he was in our intensive care unit with a self-inflicted gunshot to the head.

What a dramatic statement about the need for support. This incident occurred at the beginning of the AIDS epidemic when there was overwhelming fear and dread surrounding this disease —and the diagnosis was a death sentence. I felt compelled to start a group to hopefully avoid a repeat situation like that of Mr. W. At that time, health care workers were reluctant to care for these patients, as many of them were afraid of contracting the disease. Grady established an AIDS Clinic in 1986 to serve all but the only space found was a room in the back of the Employee Health Clinic. The clinic continued to grow and expand over the years and it now has its own freestanding building.

Group Formation:
The early stages of the group's formation focused on practical matters such as the recruitment of members, marketing the group, and getting the buy-in of the medical/nursing staff in the AIDS clinic. Once I had identified several prospective group members, the next challenge was finding a suitable meeting room (space is a valuable commodity in hospitals). The only available, somewhat suitable space was a

conference room owned by Chaplaincy. They allowed me to use the room one hour per week on Fridays —the clinic only met on Fridays at that time, so this was perfect. The room provided considerable privacy as there were no windows —and very poor ventilation —but we had a space. I was able to get complimentary bag lunches from our cafeteria (bologna and cheese sandwiches with a beverage). Once we began, the group continued for close to ten years and as the clinic's population grew, we began meeting in space owned by the clinic. We kept the meeting at a consistent time and day —but the lunches were elevated to ham and cheese (thanks to the Head of Food Service at the time).

Following all of my training in "group work" at Howard, I started out with a particular protocol in mind. Potential group members were interviewed individually to determine their suitability, and they were given some idea of what to expect in the group. There was no particular restriction on who could participate – it just turned out that the group's composition was made up of gay males (and initially mainly Caucasian). The group was open to anyone who was a patient in our clinic. Initially, having an "open group" presented no problem; however, once the group developed and the core membership was established, I wanted to "close" the group. The group members solidly pushed back on the idea of closing the group as their sentiment was this: "anyone suffering from AIDS should be able to join the group" so the group remained open. The group members were willing to risk their anonymity in order to keep the group open. The average attendance through the years ranged anywhere from six to ten members. However, there were a few sessions when we had as many as eighteen to twenty participants. Even when we had that many participants on occasion, the core members dominated the discussion. Over the years, I became much more flexible with the "rules" for the group. For example, since it became an open group, I stopped the pre-interview of members as it became impossible.

Group Facilitation:
From the beginning, I always had a co-facilitator. The social worker assigned to work in the AIDS clinic was my co-facilitator over the years.

I continued my administrative duties along with my work in the group. Near the end of the group cycle, my co-facilitator was a white, gay male —and we worked very well together. Our styles were different but complementary. He was more theoretical and generally non-directive, while I tended to be directive and active in the group's deliberations.

However, we agreed on the broad purposes of the group:
1. Increasing the patients' general awareness of themselves and knowledge about their illness;
2. Assisting them in adjusting to the illness and its impact on their lives overall;
3. Providing practical support and tools for living with HIV;
4. Offering a supportive climate for positive interaction with other group members.

The group always started at noon and lasted for one hour. We had a general format for most meetings: Introductions if there were new members; "checking in" with the group (members expressed how they were feeling-emotionally, physically, etc.), and the following discussion covered whatever issues were raised from the check-in concerns. Essentially, there were no established agenda items. I would always "tune in" to the spoken and unspoken messages raised during the check-in time, listen for commonalities, major dilemmas, or interpersonal problems. Often a question was posed to all group members based on what was heard in the check-in and this generally got the group discussion going.

From time to time, based on specific issues presented by members, we invited speakers or held educational sessions around various topics. For example, the medical director of the clinic came to talk about various clinical trials and the treatment modalities being offered at the clinic at that time. At the close of each meeting, I normally summarized the discussion and highlighted the takeaways. The intent was to provide some statements that would provide insight and continued reflection. In the early days of the epidemic, the Director of Nursing was invited to a session to listen to group members describe how they felt disrespected by staff —and being a very compassionate person, she offered her intention to make the situation improve-and over time, the situation did improve.

Group Themes and Issues:

In the beginning, the group consisted mainly of white gay males (in fact, there was only one Black male for the first year and he always sat next to me). The themes at that time related more to acceptance of the illness and the fear of suffering and dealing with loss - loss of employment, loss of loved ones, and the loss of good looks. As the group's composition shifted to a primarily African-American group, some of the issues changed. Although non-acceptance by the religious community was a common theme for both, it became more prevalent among black group members. The change in the economic status of the members also paralleled the shift in the racial makeup of the group. In the early stages, the focus was on estate planning and how to live a more modest lifestyle with a reduced income. In the later stages of the group, the emphasis was on educating members about housing and welfare resources. It should be emphasized, however, that there was no apparent racial divide among members as the bond of the illness cemented the relationships of all members.

Confidentiality:

Confidentiality was discussed briefly at the beginning of every session. Some sensitive issues and tests of confidentiality arose from time to time. For example, since we initially used the chaplaincy space, several requests came in from student chaplains to "sit-in" on group meetings. They had to be denied. Later, when the group began to meet in the AIDS Clinic conference room, staff members had to be told they could not just drop in to visit unless they were specifically invited.

Confidentiality was a prevalent issue as long as group members insisted on keeping the group open. However, new members did not have to reveal any pertinent information about themselves until they felt comfortable. This explains our pain when a married man came to the group for three sessions and would only give his first name. He dropped out after those few sessions and we never saw him again. He could not be contacted.

Group members often spoke of times when their confidentiality had been breached. One member from a rural Georgia town revealed that his doctor had informed his estranged wife of his diagnosis. He felt very betrayed and was encouraged by the group to seek legal action.

There were a couple of occasions when I would encounter members in events around town. I purposely would not approach them unless they acknowledged me first —and this seemed to work well.

Family Issues:
The issues surrounding family relationships were paramount. Acceptance or non-acceptance of a gay lifestyle was a continuing concern. Several members were totally estranged from their families and sought to establish an alternative family support system. In this sense, the group took on a special meaning for those members. Members were encouraged to exchange phone numbers and offer support to one another outside of the meetings. If a regular member missed one or two meetings —someone would routinely check on that member. Almost to a person, those members who were estranged from their natural families would speak about the "hurt and pain" being ostracized caused them. Most held out hope that their families would rethink their position and welcome them back into the family.

Intimacy versus Isolation:
Much discussion centered around the need for companionship versus remaining isolated. Most members expressed concern about passing the virus to someone else even when practicing "safer sex." We did a lot of role-playing to help resolve many of the issues in this arena. The group set some standards for themselves and dealt harshly with anyone who seemingly was not practicing safe sex. It should be mentioned that we had a member newly arrived in the city who openly spoke of his loneliness and the desire for companionship and he attended several meetings. Early one Saturday morning, I received a phone call. This member had been savagely murdered by someone he had invited into

his home. At the next meeting, we discussed the circumstances of the murder as a "teachable moment" for others as to how they could take care and conduct themselves in the future.

Fear of Suffering and Dependency:
Before beginning the group, I anticipated that the focus would be on the fear of dying. However, I quickly learned that members had a greater fear of suffering and being a burden on someone. Members were encouraged to complete advanced directives and to have discussions with their doctors about their wishes. Initially, I planned to have members visit whenever a member was hospitalized - but I discovered that members were reluctant to visit the hospital. I then realized that the hospital visits reminded them of what was ahead for all of them. So instead, I made the visits and reported back to the group.

Spirituality and Religion:
Issues relating to religion and spirituality were constant themes. The general perception among white members was that they had a large degree of acceptance from their religious institutions-with some pockets of resistance. On the other hand, the black members spoke of condemnation and hostility from the black church, with great anguish and pain. Many spoke of the hypocritical nature of some of the local religious leaders, as they knew of "closet" gays within those ranks. I distinctly remember on occasion when members started naming local church leaders who were gay —and I immediately stopped the calling out of names-and reminded them that they would not want someone to do that to them.

Group Profiles:
Several patients had a major impact on the group and I wish I could profile all of them, but I have chosen to select only three of them. These three patients were active members until their deaths (and they were very special to me). Real names of those profiles are not used.

Dennis was a white gay male in his early forties. He was a former executive at one of the leading banks in the country, married to the "storybook southern belle" and the father of two teenage sons. By his own account, that life caused him misery as he was living a "lie." Even with his diagnosis, he felt relieved of pressure and was pleased to have moved away from all of the traditional middle-class trappings. Yet he often spoke of the pain of not being allowed to have contact with his sons and the fact that his family of origin had also disowned him. All of this made the group especially meaningful to him.

He poured his heart and soul into the group's development-- organizing lists of members, tracking absent members, organizing special events, etc. Perhaps his most important contribution was the extent of his "sharing" in the group —and this seemed to inspire others to follow suit. He took it upon himself to bring a closing item to each meeting —an inspirational poem or a special reading of some kind. He never missed a single meeting for two years until he moved to another city -and he would still visit periodically.

Dennis and I developed a special bond. He taught me so much about being gay and the painful price he paid. He gave a presentation to the entire social work staff on one occasion —and as he told his life story almost everyone in the audience was in tears. When he observed the expressions of sadness—he immediately told them to "stop crying as he had done enough of that already." He was admired and respected by the group for his intellect, his ability to relate to all members, his sense of humor, and his compassion for all of the members. I was able to visit him in the hospital just before he died (he knew his time had come). He joked about what the nurses were probably saying about me visiting "a gay white guy." His one hope was that his sons would visit before he passed —his ex-wife had agreed to let them visit. He died three days after my visit as I was on his notification list.

Phil was not a Grady patient but had been referred by a social work colleague in another state. He was the oldest member of the group and came with the idea that this was something to do while he awaited death. He had researched the disease and was sure that being in his 60s had sealed his fate-and he would die soon. Phil was a professional social worker who struggled with whether he could be open about his sexuality. Despite his training, he was not prone to put on his social work hat in the group and attempt to lead in any way —but he was very supportive of the group process. The group gave him the courage to be true to himself and I saw him transform from an uptight three-piece suit guy to one who comfortably began wearing turtlenecks with necklaces.

Dennis was especially helpful to Phil as they were both high achievers in their professions and both had strained family relationships. A major hurdle for Phil was informing his adult children of his HIV status. His disclosure to his family came after much work in the group and even some role-playing as to how it might be handled. The group was very focused on this event in his life and celebrated when he reported telling his family without encountering the rejection he had expected. Another major event in his life was the birth of a grandson. This event seemed to give him a new lease on life and his goal was to live for the child's first birthday. He lived to see the child enter elementary school and credited the group with having saved his life —and he gave me a big boost when he put me at the top of the saving list.

Then, there was Jay —a stark contrast to most of the group members. He was a streetwise hustler who preferred to be called "Pam" and was well accepted in the group, despite his educational level and flamboyant style. He was in and out of jail for various reasons, including petty theft and public drunkenness. Pam would often talk about his sexual exploits —and the group would plead with him to change some of his risky behaviors. Despite the group condemnation of his behavior, Pam recognized the group cared about him. He never left the group but his bragging about his risky behavior lessened over the years. Whenever he would miss a meeting, he would call and provide a reason. I will always remember when he announced to the group that he was about to die —and he described how he wanted to be buried in a "red dress" and that he would watch over me up in Heaven. My co-leader at the time had to leave the room he was so upset with this news —others were upset as well but assured Pam they would be there for him until the end. Several of us attended his graveside service and it was there that I learned that his mother had lost another son to this same illness.

The group helped me to grow as a person and as a professional. I learned a great deal about the medical aspects of the disease process, but I learned even more about the psychosocial aspects of the disease. I learned to be more accepting of people whose lifestyles might be different from mine, but who possess the same desires and hopes as anyone else in society. I gained a better understanding of what it means to have a "good death" and how I could assist patients in that regard. I learned to adapt and change in meaningful ways to help my members. Group members insisted on calling the group a "therapy" group and in many respects, it did provide therapy for them.

When various group members would give me treasured items as they were approaching their final days —I would accept these items because it meant so much to them. The value of these items was minimal —but enormous in meaning to these members —many of the photos, earrings, and the like I kept for years. I was even given a chair by one member and kept it in my basement for years, as it matched nothing in my house. All of the group members are now deceased, but will always be remembered by me for their giving spirit and courage in dealing with a terminal illness that caused them to be ostracized by many. The group provided me the most treasured experience of my entire professional career, and for that, I am truly grateful to all "my guys."

This is an edited reprint based on an article written by Charlene Turner and previously published. It is used here with permission from Taylor & Francis Group: Barbara I Willinger, Alan Rice. A History of AIDS Social Work in Hospitals: A Daring Response to an Epidemic| Edn. 1. Binghamton, NY, Haworth Press, 2003.

THE NEED FOR A SOCIAL ADMIT

Venita Griffin Brown

The social worker's role is to assess and give input to the treatment plan. In our assessment, we are looking at everyone's behavior, the individual pathology, and the whole. We try to get a picture of the patient individually and their family system, the strengths and weaknesses. We work toward the betterment of the identified patient and aim to bring about an improvement in the family system.

That said, I remember working with an 82-year-old patient and her family, during the last years of my tenure as the geriatric clinic social worker at Grady. I met her one Friday afternoon when she arrived for her scheduled appointment accompanied by her 55-year-old daughter and caregiver. Her daughter was sad and emotionally distraught. My patient lived with her daughter and son-in-law in their home. She was now in the stage of her Alzheimer's disease where she was getting her days and nights mixed up, sleeping most of the day, and staying up most of the night. Her behavior consisted of rambling through drawers and closets and roaming the house, attempting to live out memories of her yesteryears. This meant she was getting dressed for work and trying to get outside to catch the bus to go to work.

My patient's daughter opened up and very tearfully shared that she and her husband had been arguing daily about her mother's behaviors - not sleeping at night and trying to leave the house throughout the night. She was keeping everyone in the house up, rambling through drawers, and taking objects to try to open the doors of the house to get outside. Her daughter requested that we find a nursing home placement. She expected that her mother would be placed right away, within a couple of hours of their arrival at the geriatric clinic. My patient's daughter went on to tell the doctor that her husband gave her an ultimatum, do something with her mother or he would leave the marriage. She was not to bring her mother back to their home.

I intervened and met with the patient and her daughter, to explain to them the process for a patient to be placed in a nursing home. I emphasized with the daughter that a nursing home placement is not a quick, immediate, or same-day process. I explained the considerations to determine if a nursing home placement is needed and in the best interest of the patient. The patient's daughter cried and said she didn't know what to do because she couldn't return home with her mother.

Realistically, it would probably be another 7-10 days before the patient could actually be accepted in a nursing home, but definitely not on the same day, not on that day, the day of her mother's geriatric clinic appointment. The patient's daughter left out of the exam room telling me that she needed to use the bathroom in the lobby of the clinic waiting room. She went to the restroom, but when she came out, she told the clinic receptionist that she needed to go put money in the parking meter and she would be back.

My patient's daughter did not return to the clinic before we closed that day at 4:30 PM. She left her mother for us to decide the best next step for her. The doctor called the daughter's cell phone, to no avail, as she did not answer. For at least an hour, both the doctor and I tried to reach the patient's daughter by telephone. Finally, the doctor wrote an order for the patient to be a "social admit" to the hospital. I was duty-bound to make an Adult Protective Service Report about the incident, as my patient's daughter had abandoned her.

After 5:00 PM that day, Security came to the Geriatric Clinic to report to our nurse and doctor that my patient's daughter had fallen out in the elevator on the ground floor. After returning to the clinic and finding the door locked, lights off, and the blinds closed, she passed out. Security reported that she told them, she was looking for her mother. She explained that she had left her, abandoned her because her husband told her she better not come back home with her mother. He threatened to leave her. Security informed us that my patient's daughter was transported to the ER by stretcher for medical attention that as he reported, it seemed she desperately needed. From this patient, my work with the entire family began.

MENTAL ILLNESS OR JUST HUMAN?

Venita Griffin Brown

My fondest memory at Grady Hospital during my tenure as a psychiatric social worker was working with a 58 years old schizophrenic black lady. Her 33-year-old daughter, who resided with her in Public Housing, came to her mother's mental health therapy session. She reported her mother was not doing so well and suggested that I should speak to her mother's psychiatrist about admitting her for psychiatric evaluation. One of the things she reported was that once a year for about an entire week her mother would sit in the bathtub, without any water in the tub. Now, her mother had done this the past week <u>and</u> she was constantly smiling very gleefully, <u>and</u> talking to herself.

I met with the patient individually to assess her, and to better analyze this reportedly unusual behavior, as reported by her daughter. I explained her daughter's concerns. The patient smiled and stated, she guessed she should have taken her clothes off in the tub. She recalled that as a little girl her mother would always run her bathwater, and help her to get undressed when it was bath time. I met with the patient and her daughter together and told them I would not recommend psychiatric hospitalization. Her daughter looked very puzzled. I shared my assessment that her mother was likely grieving the loss of her mother. Her behavior reflected her reminiscing when her mother would bathe her as a child. I surmised that this behavior occurred around her mother's birthday or during her birthday week. The patient was experiencing the grief process and in her unique way, expressing how much she missed her mother and wished she was still with her.

I have learned not to define a mentally ill patient solely by their axis 1 diagnosis. I look deeply to see their humanity. I make sure I listen to them and pay attention to their emotions, irrespective of how they choose to express them.

POSTSCRIPT

THE MIRACLE WORKERS

Kimberly D. Manning, MD

I saw this woman once in clinic. It was December and she'd caught two buses to reach us just to get her blood pressure checked and to get her medication refills. And at the end of that visit we were talking about the holidays and such and she let me know that Christmas used to be her favorite but now wasn't. And I won't belabor this with some elaborate tale but instead will go ahead and cut right to the predictable chase and let you know that it had to do with her financial situation. She had an eleven year old daughter and a nine year-old son who wouldn't get a single gift because she couldn't afford it.

Yeah.

But they had food and a warm home, you know? And she seemed cool with all of that. Like, she wasn't all super melancholy or mad dramatic about it. It just was what it was. And even that--the fact that this was her normal and clearly she'd figured out how to navigate it--isn't the point. I really tell you this to tell you about something else that happened after this encounter.

Oh.

And let me just preface this by saying that what happened after that encounter wasn't exotic or unusual at all. Instead it was something that happens on a daily basis in hospitals like Grady all over the country.

Yup.

I called our social worker. And all I did was tell her about this woman and her situation. Then, like our social workers do, she came over to the patient and sat down and spent time finding out her situation.

Next thing I knew, some community resources were identified that happened to service the area right where my patient lived. And they were willing and also able to help this woman give her kids just a little bit of magic on Christmas morning.

Yep.

It was short notice. We were like three days shy of Christmas, so that social worker went to wherever she got those resources, retrieved some gift cards and personally went out and bought things for those children herself. Then she delivered it to my patient's home along with some stuff for her to present it to her kids as gifts.

She sure did.

A man I cared for on the hospital service had been ill and was estranged from his family due to a multi-year drug stronghold. He'd been unstably housed and mostly on his own or in the streets. But this illness was serious and sidelined him in that way that no one ever wants to be sidelined. "Where are your people?" I asked. And I asked that because in a place like Georgia everyone has "people." Or even "peoples" as some folks say. Anyway. This man said he did have people but that he didn't know where they were or how to reach them. The names were patched all together in a ragged little tapestry that fractured into pieces the minute any of us tried to pull it all together.

But.

Then I told the social worker. And that social worker stepped in and got to work. And if you work at a place like Grady or have had any contact with a great and dedicated social worker, you know that there is no need to even say "spoiler alert" before anything else. She found that man's people. And his peoples, too. And those folks were worried and glad and thankful to be able to come to the side of their family member during that time.

Now.

Finding somebody's people or peoples may not seem like a big deal to you but it is. And when things like drug addiction and untreated mental health issues and time stand as looming barriers, many times it's a downright miracle when those pieces get put together. And even more of a miracle when something right and good happens as a result.

But this--these sorts of ordinary miracles--happen every single day at Grady. And in this moment I am reflecting on our social workers-- the miracle workers--who open the doors and windows that have been painted shut for so many for so long. I cannot do what I do without them. The obstacles are too great; my caring alone is not enough.

Earlier this month, one of my favorite Grady social workers of all time died. She fell ill swiftly and was gone in the twinkling of an eye. And when I heard the news it truly broke a piece of my heart. Truly, it did. Because she was my friend. Or rather, we were very friendly. And I realized that I loved her. And no, not in the *eros* sense but something different. More like some hybrid between the brother-sisterly *philos* love and the nebulous *agape*-type love that one experiences spiritually. Somewhere in my deep appreciation for the selfless contributions of every single social worker I've known through the years, my heart felt a particular sadness at this loss because of that love.

Yes. That.
I am.

You know? I told Veronica how much I appreciated her every single time I called her or saw her. Not because I foresaw this, but just because it was how I felt and she always gave me space to be honest. I take some solace in that. I do. But I guess today, I felt the need to go and tell it on the mountain. Not just how thankful I am for Mrs. Smallwood, but instead putting a bullhorn to my lips to shout to the world who the *real* miracle workers are in a place like Grady. In a place dedicated to serving the undeserved? It's *them*. The ones stealthily making dollars out of fifteen cents day after day after day and leaping from often dilapidated buildings in a single bound--the social workers.

The bible says, "The greatest among you will be your servant." (Matt 23:11.)

*And shout out to Mrs. Valerie Beasley and Mrs. Dorothy Ziemer, respectively--the two miracle workers who made things happen in the two 100% true stories above.

****
excerpted from the blog, "gradydoctor"
by Kimberly D. Manning, MD
Reflections Of A Grady Doctor, Wednesday, October 28, 2015

Dr. Manning is a practicing physician at Grady Memorial Hospital in Atlanta. She is a pediatrician and is board certified in internal medicine. A graduate of Meharry Medical College School of Medicine, she has been the recipient of numerous teaching awards including the 2012 Evangeline Papageorge Distinguished Teaching Award—Emory University School of Medicine's highest recognition for teaching and most recently, the 2017 ACGME Courage to Teach Award.

HEAVEN'S ANGELS

Charlene Turner

One of the CEOs who initially wanted to almost eliminate our department said to me one day as I was leaving his office that "Grady Social Workers will have a special place in Heaven." Therefore, it is important that I offer some tribute to each one of these angels.

Kay Holloway was a supervisor who mentored a number of social workers assigned to the Medicine Service. She was like the department mascot as her influence and strong personality were felt throughout the hospital. She took a leading role in starting the Long Stay Board, researched all the cases prior to each meeting and generally provided resolutions as to how we could handle the most difficult, complex discharges. She would often work overtime to prepare for the next Long Stay Board meeting. She was diligently working to prepare her next presentation one Wednesday evening when I left the office. Early the next day, we received a call that she had passed away the night before. Her death sent shock waves throughout the hospital, as she was so loved and respected. Her portrait hangs on the wall in a room named in her honor in the Social Service Department.

Darryl Brown was one of my early hires —and one of our hardest, dedicated workers. She would habitually arrive early and go directly to her assigned area, the Burn Unit, where she would normally spend the whole day. She worked diligently despite her illness and gained the respect of the entire medical/nursing staff on the unit. To honor her memory, the unit proudly hung a plague on the floor in her name.

Mike Chambers started in the department as a student intern. He was truly a "hippie social worker" and spoke freely about his time as a "real hippie." He was unconventional in his dress. Getting him to wear socks was the initial issue; but an even greater battle arose over his refusal to wear neckties. He even brought me an article, which outlined the negative effects of wearing ties. All the male social workers tried to convince him to wear a tie. They all failed miserably. It should be noted that our hippie social worker would take on cases that others would refuse. He volunteered to work "the TB caseload", when others refused. He visited some out of the way places in town when we needed to place our first AIDS patients in a motel. He visited that patient weekly when most workers would have been afraid to frequent that area.

Hank Selinger worked as an editor at the Miami Herald before getting his social work degree. He did not have a lengthy time in the department but made an impression with his work ethic. He worked one of the department's hardest cases, which was actually made into a television movie. In the movie, he is portrayed as a psychologist. This patient was evicted from a nursing home in Ohio for his verbal abuse of staff. After considerable effort, Hank was finally able to get him into another facility.

Hank was a no-nonsense three-piece suit type of guy who happened to love baseball. He invited me to attend a Braves game with him. When he picked me up, he had transformed into a guy in some ragged cutoff shorts, sunglasses and a 'Farmer in the Dell' straw hat. I could barely enjoy the game-here I sat with this funny-looking white guy parading a huge sign that said "I hate..." (naming the Mets player he did not like). I was just hoping that no one from Grady saw us. He could also "do the James Brown" on a moment's notice as he demonstrated in my office on one occasion. He loved social work-but he also loved to have fun and he loved to dance.

Veronica Smallwood came to Grady as a student and never left. She often spoke of what Mr. Reed had taught her as a student. She was dearly loved by the medical staff on the Medicine Service as she worked hard to get the most difficult patients discharged – and the doctors used to bargain to get her on their team. The highlight of her time at Grady was when she was named the 'Social Worker of the Year' –she was the first one to receive the title.

Margaret White was one of the first social work assistants hired in the department –and she set a high bar for others who followed her. Not only did she help to mentor other social work assistants, she helped many of our MSWs learn how to negotiate the system and work effectively in the ER. While she did not have formal training as a social worker, she had a natural instinct for assessing situations and determining a course of action. Most of all –she loved people and had a genuine desire to help.

Lovelean Earl's time in the department was rather short. Still, she made an indelible impression with her colleagues in the department with her dedication and hard work, even through her illness. She worked on the Medicine Service under Kay Holloway. She was so dedicated that she continued to work, despite being ill and in a frail, weak condition. Reluctantly, taking medical leave, she passed away a week or so after leaving the job.

Nancy Miller was the primary secretary in the department for over twenty years and was instrumental in keeping records, doing payroll with upwards of 100 social workers on staff, and a myriad of other duties. She handled it all with ease. She was especially useful to me as she could type over a hundred words a minute (no computers at the time) and I wrote a lot of memos. We were so in sync that she would often finish my unfinished sentences and correct other mistakes I might have made. She kept in touch with all the social workers (even after they left). She was instrumental in coordinating a social work reunion we had in Stone Mountain in the early 90s. At that reunion, I invited everyone to come back the following year for my retirement —and then I worked for another ten years. Nancy converted me from being a tea drinker to coffee —as she would have the coffee aroma throughout the office every day — and her coffee rivals the best any coffee shop has to offer. Nancy was very loyal to me —and would bring any tidbits of information she heard in the Grady Grapevine or learned in her "smoking corner" if she felt it was something I needed to know.

Ruby Porter was close to retirement when she transferred from the Ambulance Department where she worked as a dispatcher. She worked like magic on the phone and could handle three or four calls at the same time. In addition, she had a special way of relating to every patient who came through our door - she called almost everyone "baby" or "cuz" and could make even the most upset patient calm down. She had a natural instinct in assessing people-and would even tell me about newly hired social workers in terms of whether they were going to be successful. Her predictions were correct one hundred percent of the time. In many respects, she was the "mother" of the department to staff and patients alike. She demonstrated her kind spirit on a daily basis as she worked the front desk.

Delbra Thomas was hired in the department twice. Initially, she was a supervisor in Women's Health and Rape Crises. She was an "expert" in domestic violence issues and left the department to work in that area. Obviously, she loved Grady as she returned after several years. Once again, she worked in Women's Health and several outpatient clinics. She retired from the hospital and continued to practice social work in her church and the community at large. She could be described as a consummate professional.

And then, there were other Grady social workers, who did not work directly under the Social Service Department. Nonetheless, we were the best of colleagues and worked together seamlessly on behalf of our patients. I want to pay tribute to those whom I am aware are now among "Heaven's Angels":

>Yvonne Aldridge
>Martha Christison
>Janice Coye
>Sandra Cummings
>Walter Gott
>Fernando Harrold
>Jurella Poole

I have fond memories of Martha, who practiced in Psychiatry and was a specialist in working with children traumatized by witnessing the death of a parent(s). After she retired from Grady, Martha continued, in true social work fashion, to volunteer in the community in many capacities.

Undoubtedly, there may be others that have passed on. I wish to praise all of them and the "Unnamed Grady Social Workers"-social work angels ALL. With their help, collectively, we did good work.

Blessings...

CONTRIBUTORS:

Dollmeshia Adams, MSW, LCSW, graduated from Florida A &M University, and has 40+ years of experience in the field. She was originally hired as a medical social worker at Grady in 1974; later held various supervisory positions, including working as the Assistant Director of the Social Service Department for 22 years. She retired from Grady in 2007, and returned in 2009 where she continues to work in the Cancer Center as a Community Outreach and Education Specialist.

Valeria Beasley, MSW, has been in social work for over twenty years, and recently received her graduate degree from Walden University. For most of her career, she was the lone social worker in the Primary Clinic at Grady and carried a caseload that would have been difficult for two social workers. She was recognized for her ability to make quick assessments and decide on a course of action and to ultimately maneuver through a maze of community resources to benefit her patients. Many colleagues would seek her guidance when there was a need to identify and/or obtain needed agency/community resources. She was selected Social Worker of the Year in 2005.

Venita Griffin Brown, MSW, graduated from Wayne State University. She started work at Grady as a psychiatric social worker in 1989, left for one year and returned in 1990 as a medical social worker. She then worked in several different areas; Neurology, the Emergency Room, and the Geriatric Clinic. She retired from Grady in 1917, and presently works part-time for Community Friendship.

Dorothy F. Carrillo, MSW, LCSW, PhD, is a retired associate professor of social work who served on the faculty of the University of Georgia and Georgia State University. Previously she was a social work practitioner with over 25 years of experience in medical and school social work, group work, substance abuse, and family therapy. She was employed at Grady from 1970 – 1973. Carrrillo holds a BA from Augusta College, a MSW from Clark Atlanta University, and a doctorate from the University of Georgia. She has been retired since 2013, but actively volunteers her time whenever called upon to further the cause of social work.

Darcell Colbert, MSW, obtained her undergraduate degree from Tuskegee University, and her graduate degree from Clark Atlanta University. She worked at Grady for 20+ years and during that time covered numerous areas: the Burn Unit, Trauma, Orthopedics, Medical and Surgical ICU, Neurology and the Dialysis Clinic. She is probably best identified as the Morehouse Medicine Team Social Worker where she worked for years. She retired from Grady in 2016 and presently works part-time in a Medicaid Outreach Program.

Sonya Cruel, MSW, is a graduate of Clark Atlanta University with nearly 30 years of experience in the field. She has worked in a number of areas and has expertise in hospital program administration and grant writing in addition to her direct care with oncology patients and on mother/baby units. Under her leadership, Grady's First Steps program was recognized as one of the best in the State. She has authored two books - <u>Divorce in the Upper Room</u> and <u>Transitions: From Then To Now To Next</u>. She has also been certified as a life coach in the sphere of life transitions. She presently works in the public education system.

Patti Hammonds-Greene, MSW, PhD, received her MSW from Ohio State and her doctorate from Clark Atlanta with a specialization in administration. She came to Grady in 2001 and continues to work there part-time. During her full time work at the hospital, she worked on the Burn Unit with both children and adults. She was responsible for counselling, case management, and discharge planning.

Estella Moore, MSW, ACSW, LCSW, received her MSW from Temple University and worked at the Children's Hospital in Philadelphia prior to coming to Grady in 1982. While at Grady, she covered a variety of services: Orthopedics, Cardiology, Sickle Cell and Pediatrics. Prior to leaving Grady in 1999, she became the Manager of the Rape Crises Program, the Healthy Mothers: Best Start Program and also supervised the social workers assigned to the OB/GYN Service.

Nancy Moore, MSW, LCSW, received her MSW from the University of Connecticut. Prior to coming to Grady in 2010, Nancy worked in a number of agencies in supervisory/ management roles. She worked for Family Services of Boston and directed their counselling program. She came to Grady from Families First where she had worked as the Director of Counselling for over ten years. Her 30+ years of experience in counselling and supervision enabled her to adapt quickly to the Surgical Intensive Care Unit At Grady as her primary assignment and she continues to work there now part-time.

Vickie Ogunlade, MSW, LCSW, PhD, received her MSW from the University of North Carolina and her doctorate from Clark Atlanta University, and she has a Certification in Mindfulness Based Stress Reduction. Her social work career spans 40 years in various settings, including medical and mental health settings as well as in higher education. She has facilitated workshops and done scholarly presentations in the U.S. as well as in Nigeria. She is recognized for her level of expertise in numerous areas, including crises intervention, life transitions and grief counselling, support for survivors of trauma and abuse of all kinds —to name just a few.

Judy Plecko, MSSW, LCSW, ACSW, obtained her social work degree from the University of Texas. She has extensive clinical experience with children, adolescents and adults and has worked in private practice and in various hospital settings, including Elks Aidmore, Dekalb Medical, and Shepherd Spinal Center. She also worked at the Marcus Institute at Emory for many years where she was the Director of Family Support and Social Work. She was the Chief of Pediatric Social Work at Grady from 1972 to 1975. She has also worked as Adjunct Professor at Georgia State School of Social Work.

James Reed, Jr., MSW, JD, worked at Grady for decades (1978-2014) where he started as a staff social worker in the Cardiac Clinic. His expertise in counselling and crises intervention eventually led to his supervision of social work in the Emergency Room and the Surgery Service and promotion to the position of Director of Social Service a few years before he left Grady. He possessed a unique style of mentorship in the training of social work interns and worked dutifully as a field instructor for all of the local schools of social work. He obtained his MSW from the University of Georgia.

Phyliss A. Sanders, MSW, LCSW, received her graduate degree from Clark Atlanta and began her career at Grady in 1973 where she worked for ten years. Once she left Child Psychiatry at Grady, she held a number of supervisory/ management positions in the mental health field, including work at Emory, West Fulton Mental Health Center and Dekalb Community Services Board. She also worked as Adjunct Professor at Emory and Morehouse School of Medicine. Currently, she works with United Healthcare as a Life Coach.

Sandra Sanders, MSW, LCSW, her graduate degree was obtained from Clark Atlanta University and her tenure at Grady began in 1998 and continues to this day. She has considerable experience in dealing with patients and families who were treated in Grady's Emergency Room. Her more recent experience is focused on outpatients who frequent one of the hospital's satellite clinics. It should be noted that Sandra conducts a preparatory class for social
workers who are seeking to obtain their license –and feedback from her students indicate that they are well equipped to take the exam after completing her class.

Taryn L. Siddiq, MSW, graduated from Clark Atlanta University and worked at Grady from 1994 until 1999. She covered several different areas and became the Coordinator of Neurology Social Services. She is the founder of a nonprofit agency, Muslimah Connection Group, Inc., which focuses on the emotional and psychological needs in the transitions of life. The agency also provides consultation and training and professional development in many areas. She presently works at Emory University in the Rehabilitation Department.

Louise Spiro, MSW, LCSW, received her MSW from Clark Atlanta University and was the first social worker hired in the newly established Geriatrics Clinic at Grady. She has over 30 years of social work experience in various settings, including private practice and group work-and was the assigned social worker for the Dialysis Clinic at Grady when it closed. She continues to work with several metro area Probate Courts by doing assessments for guardianships.

V. Patricia Tatro, MSW, LCSW, did her graduate work at the University of Georgia and came to Grady in 1991 as an intern where she was assigned to the Mother/Baby Unit. After her internship, she was hired to work in that area and stayed until 1995. Social work was her second career and she continues in the field as a social worker in the Children's Hospital of Atlanta.

Claudia Taylor, MSW, MDiv, received her MSW from Clark Atlanta and her Master of Divinity from Mercer University. She began her employment at Grady in 2007 and currently works there in the outpatient area. She has also worked in the Emergency Room and the Inpatient areas. Her combined skill set has enabled her to offer counselling and support when dealing with grief and loss from both perspectives.

Charlene Turner, MSW, ACSW, LCSW, received her graduate degree from Howard University where she specialized in group work. She worked as a psychiatric social worker in Chicago prior to being hired at Grady in 1972. She worked at Grady until the end of 2013 primarily as the Director of Social Services and was promoted to the position of Administrative Director of Care Management where she supervised nurse case managers as well as social workers. She also worked as adjunct professor at Clark-Atlanta University and presently works at the Healing Community Center in Behavioral Health.

Natasha Worthy, MSW, received her Masters from Clark Atlanta University and worked at Grady from 2001 until 2005 in the Mother/Baby Unit. She continued in this area of social work and worked for years as the Program Coordinator for the Center for Black Women's Wellness.

Dorothy Ziemer, MSW, a graduate of Clark Atlanta University who worked in a variety of settings, including the Medical College of Georgia and Warm Springs prior to coming to Grady in 1989. She became the Coordinator of AIDS Social Work until 2017 when she retired. She continues to volunteer for the Infectious Disease Program at Grady. She has also served on the National Board for NASW.

Made in the USA
Columbia, SC
12 February 2021